.RY

D0200587

THE POWER OF AWARENESS

ALSO BY DAN SCHILLING

Alone at Dawn

The Battle of Mogadishu

THE POWER
OF
AWARENESS

*And Other Secrets from the World's Foremost
Spies, Detectives, and Special Operators on How
to Stay Safe and Save Your Life*

DAN SCHILLING

GRAND CENTRAL
PUBLISHING

NEW YORK   BOSTON

Grand Central Publishing
Hachette Book Group
1290 Avenue of the Americas, New York, NY 10104
grandcentralpublishing.com
twitter.com/grandcentralpub

First Edition: June 2021

Grand Central Publishing is a division of Hachette Book Group, Inc. The Grand Central Publishing name and logo is a trademark of Hachette Book Group, Inc.

The publisher is not responsible for websites (or their content) that are not owned by the publisher.

The Hachette Speakers Bureau provides a wide range of authors for speaking events. To find out more, go to www.hachettespeakersbureau.com or call (866) 376-6591.

Library of Congress Cataloging-in-Publication Data
Names: Schilling, Dan, author.
Title: The power of awareness : and other secrets from the world's foremost spies,
   detectives, and special operators on how to stay safe and save your life / Dan Schilling.
Description: New York : Grand Central Publishing, [2021] | Includes bibliographical
   references and index.
Identifiers: LCCN 2020054049 | ISBN 9781538718674 (hardcover) |
   ISBN 9781538718698 (ebook)
Subjects: LCSH: Danger perception. | Situational awareness.
Classification: LCC BF323.D36 S35 2021 | DDC 153.7/5—dc23
LC record available at https://lccn.loc.gov/2020054049

ISBN: 978-1-5387-1867-4 (hardcover), 978-1-5387-1869-8 (ebook)

Printed in the United States of America

LSC-C

Printing 1, 2021

For Julie,
who's done much to make the world safer for the many

CONTENTS

CONTENTS

THE ASSASSIN

NOTE: The names, location, and mission in the following story are masked due to certain sensitive national security considerations.

Somewhere on the Arabian Peninsula

Billy Sole sat in the passenger seat of a dusty SUV observing as the mission went down several hundred yards away. The sun was bright, almost blinding, its rays magnified by the glare of the nearby Arabian Sea. It was midsummer hot, and the ocean provided no relief, but at least their vehicle was air-conditioned. Technically speaking, Billy, a thirtysomething Air Force special operations veteran from one of America's "black" (operating under highly restricted congressional oversight) Special Mission Units, wasn't directly involved in the nearby operation. He and his three compatriots were there in case the man executing the clandestine mission should somehow come under threat from Al Qaeda.

Dressed in jeans and a well-worn collared shirt, Billy shifted in his seat, trying to get comfortable despite the Glock 19 shoved into the small of his back. At his feet lay a go bag with a compact H&K MP7 machine pistol and body armor, in case things went sideways. He watched for trouble up and down the busy road where they were parked. The locals were bustling along on the commercial strip, going about the daily business of trying to make a living in a dusty city by the sea. The heat tempered the foot traffic, even though this part of the city was something of a social destination. It was a little boring conducting overwatch for a clandestine mission— nothing ever happened, which was exactly the point of clandestine work.

Parked along the side of the road, wedged in between a line of nondescript cars, they blended in with the mix of private and commercial traffic. The locals took no notice of the men, who went to some lengths to ensure what was visible from the outside of the SUV was nondescript. This included not wearing sunglasses, because sunglasses would draw attention in this country.

The driver observed a cab pull up a car length and a half behind them and double-park. When no one got out, he mentioned it to Billy and the other two occupants, all of whom took note but paid little attention. After nearly a minute the lone passenger hadn't emerged, so Billy cast a discreet backward glance, but gleaned nothing other than the passenger was taking his time, arguing over the taxi fare or perhaps completing a phone call.

Billy turned his attention instead to a secret electronic device his team was using for targeting terrorists. The four men in his car were the best-trained black special operators in America, and therefore the world. As he focused on the device, the hair on the back of his neck began to stand up. He looked up, but nothing had changed on the street, it was the same crowd he'd been watching for two months. The cabbie and passenger were still in their double-parked space, and he brushed off the feeling.

The team's driver announced that the passenger had exited the cab behind them but was momentarily standing in their blind spot. A moment later the cab drove past the Americans, on its way to another fare. The passenger walked up the sidewalk and passed by the side of the Americans' SUV. He stopped suddenly by the front tire of the vehicle, turned to look inside, and pulled a pistol from inside his shirt. In one swift motion he jammed it against the passenger window and fired three point-blank rounds.

Without a spared glance he turned and walked in the direction he'd come, stuffing the weapon back into his shirt, and promptly disappeared.

In the SUV there was a deafening silence after the ear-shattering explosions of the pistol shots. Glass shards were scattered both on the dash and the men from the damaged bulletproof glass that had thwarted the assassin's attempt. The assassin's window choice had merely been to ensure he killed the most important American, who would surely be sitting in the front passenger seat. But now there was another problem, and in the immediate aftermath, the team's training kicked in. Billy rapidly scanned through the windows, including the passenger glass with its neat and tight three-shot grouping, for what would come next, most likely a vehicle-borne improvised explosive to kill them all.

They needed to move. Now. To remain in place was to invite death, and despite the adrenaline and a near fatality, thanks to years of training and practice, a rush of decisions and actions immediately ensued. The driver plotted his course. One of the men made a call reporting the assassination attempt. Weapons now at the ready, the others checked for additional avenues of further attack and scanned human faces for signs indicating potential assault. With the four men on high alert, the driver quickly pulled out into traffic as they all continued scanning for the next threat. All of these actions happened in a handful of seconds. Threading their way through the stunned crowds, the men disappeared into the dust and commerce of the Arabian heat.

It was a fortunate failure, and the question the four men asked each other when they'd arrived back at their safe house was *how?* They compared their individual experiences from the time the taxi appeared, revealing that each of them had felt the same sensation as Billy—something had been wrong and each of their hackles had gone up. Even though their immediate reactions to safeguard against further attempts were appropriate, the question remained: How had they allowed themselves to become the victims of an assassination attempt? This was a critical tactical and operational consideration, the nuts and bolts of clandestine work, in the midst of their ongoing and dangerous mission.

However, the more important question was *why?* Why had four of the most highly trained clandestine special operatives in the world given power and control of their safety over to an individual with lethal intent? Understanding *why* they had willingly allowed it to happen and how to prevent it is the purpose of this book.

INTRODUCTION

Like Billy (a pseudonym) and his team, who were fortunate to survive their assassination attempt, I've spent the majority of my life and career engaging in some of the most high-risk and high-consequence activities one human can pursue. In fact, at the time of the attack, I was Billy's squadron commander. I am also a veteran of one of the most violent sustained gunfights in the past half century, which took place in the remote capital of the ill-fated East African nation that is Somalia. You may know that operation by its popular name, Black Hawk Down. It was a mission that saw 200 of my fellow airmen, soldiers, and sailors combat thousands of militia and cost 18 Americans and perhaps 1,500 Somalis their lives. The outcome of that single gunfight changed US foreign policy for decades and set in motion the events that would lead to a post-9/11 world.

While seminal, that mission was but one of many I conducted both overtly and clandestinely around the world. As a Combat Controller I've snuck into countries using aliases, slipping out again without a trace of my having passed, learned how to evade enemy patrols, resist interrogation, and escape fortified imprisonment. I spent decades jumping from aircraft as a military high-altitude/low-opening (known by the acronym HALO) parachutist and professionally rated demonstration skydiver, accumulating several thousand jumps. I've dove open- and closed-circuit systems in the frigid North Pacific and tropical Andaman Sea alike. The training to become a USAF Combat Controller is one of the longest, physically and mentally toughest, and most intellectually demanding of any special operations force in the world.

Later in my career, I established—and then served as the first commander of—two special operations squadrons, the second of which is one of the blackest Special Mission Units in the world. An organization whose mission is sensitive enough that its very name and purpose remain top-secret.

This type of life and activities are not consequence-free. Losing friends, experiencing and inflicting violence, failing to save someone's life. All of these alter and damage you. Killing people, in particular, even when justified, is a net negative life experience. It does not develop you or advance you as a human. I've struggled with all of these things and in some ways always will. As a means of managing PTSD and finding my own version of peace, I added to my military exploits what is arguably the world's most dangerous sporting activity: BASE jumping. BASE jumping, if you are unfamiliar, is a type of parachuting that removes the airplane from the equation. The sport, which is completely unregulated, enjoys a well-deserved renegade—perhaps "notorious" is a better term—reputation, since much of it touches on illegality. I've jumped from the roofs of Las Vegas hotels and 1,400-foot radio antennas, though the means by which I managed to gain access to these structures are best left unrevealed.

It is a high-energy and exciting sport but exacts a comparably high price. For the first decade I BASE-jumped, I lost at least one friend to the sport every year. BASE jumpers have a saying: "BASE-jump long enough and it will eventually kill you." An accurate assessment, and I'm certainly not immune. I once had an inexplicable wall strike after opening my parachute on a 500-foot cliff I'd jumped at least 100 times. I was lucky to survive, and that mentally threw me off my game for years. So it's safe to say I understand risks and consequences, and that goes some way in explaining why it is rare for me to BASE-jump these days.

Repeated exposure to *extreme* risks and life-threatening danger such as I've experienced can lead to *extreme* coping methods. I've seen many good men and women destroyed by the long-term effects of risk and stress, and I was one of them for some time. Self-destructive behavior and overindulgence with alcohol and drugs (legal or otherwise) are common. In the end, BASE jumping may not have been the best means to find peace, but hey, it beats the hell out of the bottom of a bourbon or pill bottle.

In my special operations profession, I had the good fortune to work with some of the best military minds and organizations in the world. Units such as my own Air Force special operations squadrons and others like Delta Force and SEAL Team Six, all of whom are foremost experts in risk calculation and mitigation. My unusual career also afforded me the opportunity to work with some remarkable people in law enforcement, from the FBI's counterterrorist and counterintelligence units as well as agents from the Commerce Department and Homeland Security Investigations. In conjunction with the CIA and NSA I spent several years staring at very difficult intelligence problems that threatened world stability. The CIA also taught me the skills needed to walk in an urban environment unnoticed and with confidence regarding both foreign intelligence services and criminals, who often use similar tactics and in some countries are one and the same. This was in addition to my own SOF (special operations forces) training.

Because of that unique career, safety and risk calculation spliced themselves into, and then became, the fabric of my DNA. And I can confidently say I've used those risk-calculation skills to save my life on multiple occasions. But I didn't start that way. Nobody does. Understanding and mitigating risk is a learned activity, but you needn't join special operations, stand atop the edge of a 500-foot-tall Vegas casino with a bundle of fabric on your back, counter terrorist plots, or try and solve existential threats like nuclear proliferation to understand them. In fact, you needn't be a professional at all to be safe in many higher-risk situations that you might easily find yourself in or to thwart potential attacks on your own life. In some circumstances, there are distinct advantages to being a nonprofessional, and I'm going to show you how to use them to thwart the bad guys.

I've created six fundamental rules that you can apply in any circumstance from the world of special operations, intelligence spooks, and world-class law enforcement agencies to keep safe. I've refined them over three decades and used them to walk well-known metropolises like Bangkok and Manhattan, traverse more exotic cities like Dhaka and Nairobi, and operate in downright dangerous and contested locations such as Mogadishu and Sana'a. Whether you're an international business traveler walking the Rive Gauche in Paris in pursuit of a night out, or a soccer parent navigating an unfamiliar part of town with a car stuffed full of distracting preteens, these rules can and will save your life.

THE RULES

As I developed these six safety rules, I came to the realization they fell into three separate categories, and this conveniently made them easier to understand and implement. I refer to these categories as Know, Prepare, and Act.

KNOW—In personal safety, knowing means truly seeing and comprehending your surroundings and what is happening in them. Unfortunately, the vast majority of people around you do not comprehend, and the purpose of this book is to ensure you are not one of them. To do that, you need to know Rule 1 (Be Situationally Aware) and Rule 2 (Trust and Use Your Intuition) and understand that they are absolutely critical. Without both, you are blind. Everything else you do to be safe builds on this dual foundation, and for that reason these rules comprise the biggest sections in the book.

PREPARE—Understanding threats and potential threats allows you to also understand whether there is something to be concerned about. And if there is, what you should do about it. This is where many people stop short of what's necessary to ensure their own safety because they don't have a deliberate process to implement. Rule 3 (Determine If You Have a Problem) and Rule 4 (Develop a Plan) allow you to shape and better determine outcomes by preparing you in the event you need to take action.

ACT—Ultimately, we must take action if we are under threat or potential threat. Rule 5 (Act Decisively) and Rule 6 (The Two Rs) are merely the final action steps in resolving or avoiding a crisis and simultaneously the easiest and possibly the most difficult. Acting decisively, if you follow the rules in this book, is the simplest. If you understand your situation and have a plan, to act is both clear and straightforward because you've already done the work. You're simply implementing that plan.

In Rule 6 (The Two Rs) you'll learn that to Regroup is to take stock immediately after a crisis to determine what, if anything, you need to do next, and also that distance equals safety. It is the second R, Recover, that many people find difficult, especially if there was violence involved. However, a key part in any return journey toward psychological and emotional well-being is to contact the authorities and to find support (professional or personal). After a crisis, we always must go on with life, and you deserve to recover to the fullest extent possible.

Throughout the Rules section of the book you'll occasionally encounter this symbol:

It's an indication to stop and either reflect on a topic or complete some item before moving on. To get the greatest benefit from this book, I encourage you to take the time to do so. If you skip the sign, you're not giving yourself the opportunity for honest self-assessment. And if you pause where indicated and complete the suggestion, you may be quite surprised by what you learn about yourself.

THE TOOLS

In addition to the rules for personal safety, I've designed six tools to increase your security in different ways. These tools are neither sequential nor synchronized but are there as resources.

Tool 1 (Preparedness) is all about being ready *before* something happens. Your home is a place for special considerations. Within its walls are contained your most important possessions as well as everything you need for safety. The key lies in understanding its strengths and weaknesses combined with impartial assessment, prudent planning, and crisis scenario rehearsal. I also explore public transportation, weapons, and self-defense training.

Tool 2 (Reducing Your Criminal Target Profile) is designed to make you aware that what you wear, how you act and even walk are all signals you transmit to the people around you. While the foundation of your safety rests with the six rules, you can do much to reduce your "target" profile by making a few simple choices.

Tool 3 (Armed Threats and Active Shooters) is a special-interest item. If you're an American it's more of a real concern than if you live in virtually any other country in the developed world. The Active Shooter Tool will help you quickly assess your situation and take action and can save your life in the unlikely and unfortunate event you find yourself in one.

In Tool 4 (Reducing Your Personal Information Footprint) you'll be shocked at just how much of your personal life you transmit through your phone or local Starbucks internet hot spot. More important, you'll come away armed with enough information to know how not to let details slip out unintended to criminals.

Tool 5 (Digital to Three-Dimensional Dating) is not about your online profile and how to meet people but what you should understand when you transition from digital interaction to a real live three-dimensional meeting. Because it's your life and it shouldn't be wasted, or risked, on the wrong person.

Tool 6 (Travel Planning)—whether for business or holiday—is there to help you with such tasks as destination assessment, hotel and room selection, tourist considerations, and dealing with emergency situations while away from home.

ART VS. SCIENCE

Many security experts view personal safety as some kind of clinical science. This is a natural thing for experts to do, allowing them as it does to demonstrate their expertise and knowledge of things esoteric. Many of these (it must be said) self-appointed experts use formulas and numbers to try and reduce everything to some sort of numeric calculation. One of the reasons I wrote this book was my repeated encounters with poorly written and self-promotional books on safety. While I am an expert on aspects of the subject of risk and safety, I know I'm not the foremost in any one topic. The key to providing the most value in this book was creating a team comprised of expert minds. Throughout my decades of special operations, everything I ever accomplished that was difficult, complex, or rewarding came about through teamwork. The best plans and ideas are realized through the collaborative process. For that reason, you'll find these pages filled with these other experts' stories and lessons.

I see personal safety as more art than science because there isn't some number or calculation or equation that you can arrive at or point to and say, "Aha! *That's* my situation. And therefore, I must do_____ [fill in the blank]." Reality is more fluid than that. You have to go with it and not fight it, but it does require you to start with a foundation. The most essential lessons on the following pages are having accurate Situational Awareness and tapping into and listening to your Intuition and reinforcing them until they become second nature. That is the art that emanates from the innate tools several million years of evolution have provided you, though they may be dormant or suppressed from living in the convenient and modern world. Everything else, and I do mean everything, flows from those two. Without them none of the other rules work. Let me restate that another way. Here are the two most important sentences of this book: **Situational Awareness and Intuition *are* your Power of Awareness. And your Power of Awareness *is* your personal safety.**

CONCLUSION

All of the above leads us to this book and what it is. And also what it isn't. This book is primarily a how-to manual and reference guide for your personal safety *before* something happens. This is not a book that needs to be read in its entirety first and then absorbed through reflection. For some people it will work better in installments, particularly Rules 1 and 2. Not only do Situational Awareness and Intuition form the foundation of the book, they are powerful tools in and of themselves, lending their value to almost any situation or goal. This book does not provide absolutes or guarantees, nor cover every situation in which you may find yourself. It does deliver sound advice and tactics mined from the rich veins of hard-earned experience.

Also, you shouldn't view the content on these pages as something you read once and then move on with your life. This material should not be reviewed and forgotten. It won't truly make a difference in your personal safety unless you come back to it and practice it in your life. That's the reason I've included exercises and why they're available for free on my website. In special operations we tend to be better at certain complex actions, such as calling in airstrikes while under fire or clearing buildings of terrorists, not because we're superior people (we're not) but because we practice and perfect these skills more than anyone else. You can do this too in your approach to your own personal safety, and I encourage you to do so and also to revisit passages of the book where you feel you could benefit most.

Most people would agree that personal safety is a serious topic. But it needn't be approached somberly. There is a story about Sigmund Freud when he had cancer later in life that I've always enjoyed. A contemporary approached him to discuss a point of psychology but in deference to Freud's condition said, "Perhaps I'd better not talk to you, because you've got this cancer which is very serious. You may not want to talk about this." To which Freud replied, "This cancer may be fatal, but it's not serious." The perfect response. For surely his cancer was not something to be dismissed, but it needn't hinder what he was engaged in at that moment by casting a somber shadow. The two were distinct and separate.

My approach to life and safety is very much in line with Freud's sentiments, at least regarding seriousness. And yours should be as well. Being overly serious or somber about your safety can lead to a type of bias and paranoia where everything can be interpreted as threats. Not only is that not reality, it's not effective either. So, it's a serious business, personal safety, but we're not going to be overly serious. Together we're going to instill confidence and a positive attitude, which are significant safety attributes in and of themselves, and this book is designed to foster both.

Outside these pages and in the real world, if you follow my rules in situations that would benefit from them, nothing will happen. That's because, by definition, you can't prove a negative. Such is the way of events with multiple variables and involving humans. I've been fortunate to have survived a number of serious experiences, avoided terrorist attacks as well as civil unrest in foreign countries, and, I've no doubt, skirted criminal intent. But how close was I really to losing my life in any of those situations? I'll never know. All that is to say, like me, you'll never actually or fully know what threats or potential threats your Situational Awareness, Intuition, and prudent actions saved you from. That's a good thing, by the way.

But enough introduction. Let's begin digging into the rules, which is the reason you picked this book up. And they start, as most beginnings do, with a story.

THE RULES

PART I

KNOW

BE SITUATIONALLY AWARE

La Salina, Old Mexico

I STOOD ON TOP OF A MOUNTAIN OVERLOOKING THE NEARBY PACIFIC Ocean. Always a relaxing view from this particular summit. It wasn't the view I'd climbed for, however, but to speed-fly a parachute from the top. It was warm and a bit humid, as it often is near the ocean in Baja California in November. I'd been in Mexico for a couple of weeks, pre-running the racecourse in advance of the legendary Baja 1000 off-road race. The race, held annually in Baja, Mexico, is arguably the most famous off-road endurance race in the world. The mountaintop flight was merely an opportunity to get a little exercise and have a bit of fun on the way to the Tijuana border crossing. Our race car, on which we'd spend the next week finalizing preparations to crush our competition, waited north of the border in San Diego.

Beside me was my good friend JT, laying out his own speedwing, casually prepping. Unlike skydiving or BASE jumping, two other sports we share a passion for, speedwings merely require spreading the canopy out on the ground and then running downslope, gaining speed till flight takes over. From there it's a terrain-hugging thrill ride to the bottom of the mountain.

In two minutes we'd be airborne, sharing the sky as we swooped back to JT's truck, affectionately nicknamed Big Red, parked at the bottom of the slope. I could see Red waiting, loaded with our pre-runner racer (basically a practice race vehicle), racing equipment, camping gear, more parachutes, and our personal belongings (passports, laptops, and the like) at the dead end of a desolate dirt road terminating at the trailhead to our launch point. Aside from half a dozen dilapidated shacks along the route, there were zero people or cars visible all the way back to Mexico Federal Highway 1, Mexico's version of the Pacific Coast Highway.

"Hey, there's a car pulling up to Big Red," JT announced.

I turned from my parachute and squinted at the tiny import sedan stopped next to our truck below. "Could be some other speedflyers or paragliders perhaps," I offered. I could see they had backed up and their trunk was open. From our summit, a mere 600 slant yards away, it was impossible to make out any useful details.

"Maybe. We should get back quick."

"Yup," I agreed and turned away to snap my wing into my harness. I'd be off this rock in sixty seconds. Left side. Right side. I bent forward, checking my risers and line groups, ensuring all was as it should be, when I heard JT behind me.

"Holy shit, they stole Big Red!"

As I jerked upright, he repeated himself. "They fucking stole Big Red!"

"Call the Federales, dude," I said as I turned. I stared in disbelief. Below me our silver flatbed, loaded with JT's race car and all our gear, was now raising a small dust trail as it followed the sedan back down the road.

"How do you call the Federales?!" he asked as he pulled out his phone.

Was 9-1-1 the number to call in Mexico during an emergency? I realized I had no idea. "I dunno," I said truthfully as I watched the disappearing truck, then added, "They saw us. They saw us with binoculars. Fuck." Because it was instantly clear they'd been tipped off and had cased us. I heard JT get on the line, "*Hola?...*" when I was thunderstruck by a sudden realization: I had things in Big Red that should not be stolen. Not my racing and camping gear, all of which could be replaced. In my haste to leave for the trip I'd placed a thumb drive in my laptop bag with files on my current book project (not this one). That drive also held my company files and tax documents. I took off my helmet, set it down (my GoPro was already on and inadvertently capturing the entire theft, including the photo below), and knelt to watch events unfold as JT explained our disappearing truck to the police. Since there was nothing I could do to stop it, I reverted to stereotypical tourist: I snapped a photo. Given my extensive specialized background, I am not, as should be clear already, a stereotypical tourist. So just how did a guy with three decades of special operations expertise let this happen? Well, read on and I'll tell ya.

On the right: Special ops badass or hapless tourist? You be the judge...

WHAT IS SITUATIONAL AWARENESS?

Putting yourself in the wrong place at the wrong time, as I did, is only part of the risk in any situation. And you needn't travel to third-world countries or war zones to find yourself in that undesirable position. It can happen in the city where you live or in your very own home. The key is to be aware, so that if something *does* happen, or is about to, you can shape the situation in a way that produces a positive outcome based on your available options. Welcome to Situational Awareness.

You probably have a preconceived notion of the term, but chances are that notion's a hazy generality of what it truly means. So, what is it? Webster's provides no answer, but Wikipedia offers this generally accepted definition used by researchers and emergency professionals: *"Situational Awareness (SA) is the perception of environmental elements and events with respect to time or space, the comprehension of their meaning, and the projection of their future status."* A solid scientific answer, but does it provide a useful interpretation for the layperson? What does that definition mean to you, the reader? In a practical sense, not much.

I prefer this version: Situational Awareness is *knowing where I am and what's around me, what's going on in my surroundings and my place in them.*

That well-stated and easily understood definition was provided by a former operator and combat veteran I'll call Dutch Schaefer who worked for me when I commanded a top-secret special operations squadron some years ago. Although it seems to be a simple concept, I encourage you to stop right now and really think about it. Think about the definition above and your place in time right now, with this book in hand or as you listen to an audio version. Where are you? What is around you? What's happening in those same surroundings and what is your place in them? In other words, how do the events and people around you relate to you and you to them? You aren't looking for threats, merely using your power of observation and awareness. All of these things combined form your Situational Awareness.

Applying these powers of observation in a useful manner is the essence of Situational Awareness because it allows you to know your place in your environment—for our purposes, particularly in regard to threats. In my profession I have used it to save my life on several occasions. Situational Awareness can be taught using simple and easily implemented tools, and like differentiating art from pornography you'll come to recognize it when you are experiencing it. That is a good thing because it is critical that you learn to see "what's there" through new eyes, to read details you never noticed and understand their significance.

An easy means of doing that came about in the course of my three decades in special operations, which taught me to reduce any subject or task to its simplest usable parts. For that reason I break Situational Awareness down into two components. First there is the situation. The type of environment you find yourself in. Are you ensconced in your home, tucked away from the larger world and surrounded by things you know and trust well? Or are you walking alone on an unfamiliar city street at two a.m.?

The second component is the level of your awareness. In the first scenario above, are you tuned out from everything around you except *Monday Night Football* or perhaps your favorite medical drama? Are you sitting contemplatively enjoying the quiet? Are you listening for sounds from your children's rooms or outside your home in the dark? For that city scenario, are you walking with your phone out, reading an email or some text thread? Or are you scanning what's around you: side streets, stoops, who's behind you, if anyone? In their own homes, people have low Situational Awareness because the environment is extremely familiar; they are happily engaged with their TV or making dinner. Contrast that with navigating a new place, especially at night, where Situational Awareness will hopefully be high as you take in all of the stimuli you need to navigate safely; you notice every passerby and turn at each noise.

One's situation is objective and external because your surroundings will be what they are regardless of how you assess or navigate them. One's awareness is subjective and internal, dependent on your ability to perceive, interpret, and shape your response to your circumstances. The extent to which you use your awareness to shape your situation determines your safety and is why Situational Awareness is the foundation of this book. In the remaining pages you will also find it referred to simply as SA, a term we use frequently in the military to describe it. While subsequent steps such as making plans and taking action are important, they all rely on the premise that you understand what's going on around you and your place in it: your situation and your awareness.

SITUATION

How do you assess your personal safety, whether you're in a new place or somewhere familiar? When you go to a movie theater, there is always an announcement that draws your attention to the exit signs; a similar announcement gets made when you board an airplane. But when you walk into a restaurant, do you think about whether there might be doors other than the one you entered from? Your Situational Awareness when going about your daily life is likely not especially high, because nobody has taught you that it should be. That's what I want to change in this chapter: not to make you paranoid or fearful but to ensure that you are paying attention. To help set a mental picture for you, below are some general situational and environmental categorizations.

Unfamiliar situations include a new hotel, strange cities, tourist destinations in foreign countries, strange streets, public transportation overseas, etc.

Safe environments are typically indoors, well lit, or provide stand-off distance from others. Restaurants or store interiors and hotel lobbies are good examples. Public beaches or parks are outdoor examples. Spaces with large numbers of people that make it difficult to attack or separate you, such as museums or sports stadiums, are also safe.

Unsafe or risky environments are typically outdoors, poorly lit, with masked passageways or choke points you have to pass through, and they may also involve groups or crowds. Choke points are places to pay particular attention to, and they come in two flavors. The first is any area you must travel through to get to a destination without alternative options. Designated parking garage entrances in multilevel structures where everyone has to park for work, for instance. Or an intersection you must pass through to get home every day. Because you can't avoid them, they are predictable locations to be followed, trapped, or ambushed. The entrance to your home or apartment complex, if it has a secure gate, is particularly vulnerable. The second type of choke points are locations that constrict your movement or force you to slow down or even stop to pass through, like the doorway of a restaurant or store. These also tend to be places that force many people toward a single spot and produce congestion or stoppages. Think of the places you're familiar with while driving that suffer from congestion, and the root cause will be choke points that force too many cars through one or a few spots in a short amount of time, such as where two lanes merge into one. Like your driving habits, your personal habits should lead you to avoid choke points whenever possible. More on this later.

Regardless of where you are, every situation combines a category with a risk element that you can rapidly assess in four combinations. Familiar and Safe. Unfamiliar and Safe. Familiar and Unsafe. Unfamiliar and Unsafe. These can be thought of as different quadrants. It may sound complex but it's not. This chart shows how easy it can be to mentally identify your situation and the attendant risk/threat:

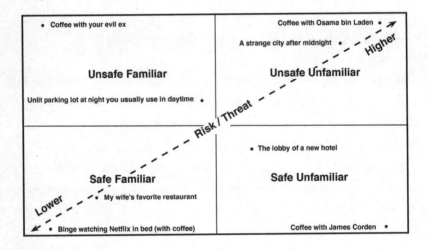

Risk/Threat Matrix

Each plotted point represents a likelihood for potential threat. It isn't important at this point to assess *what* that threat might be, such as a robbery or assault and so forth. Rather, you merely want to understand the *potential* for something to happen.

Here are a few examples from my own experiences:

Familiar and Safe: Dining at my wife's favorite restaurant in Salt Lake City near our home.

Unfamiliar and Safe: A new restaurant inside the Las Vegas hotel where I was staying to give a speech.

Familiar and Unsafe: On the streets of Bangkok, a city I know well but where I was still clearly a foreigner.

Unfamiliar and Unsafe: Walking the streets of Nairobi after midnight on my first visit.

It's an easy exercise in learning how to assess yourself and your risk and is something we'll spend more time on in this chapter.

Humans are creatures of habit, which goes some way toward explaining why we can be so unreliable when it comes to recalling details in a crisis or under stress. We often expect to see certain things, particularly in familiar surroundings. It's the blind spot you can't see because you're already blinded by familiarity. In going about daily activities in public and even higher-risk situations, you can easily be preoccupied, even without your phone (more in a moment on that topic).

When people are somewhere familiar that feels very safe and comfortable, I see them fall into what I call the "Yup, nothing's here" syndrome. This means that we're inclined to accept what we assume is true about our environment rather than taking the time to assess what's actually there. In other words, seeing what you "want" to see.

You end up being vulnerable precisely because you are so comfortable with the familiar. And most of the time this is fine: It's why you've fallen into the habit; it's a natural affiliation between you and your familiar environment, built up over time, further reinforced by iterative experience since, hey, nothing's ever happened in all that time, right? So why should it now? You see what you expect in your daily commute, at work or lunch, and around town. But what is actually there can be quite different than your preconceived notion. This tendency to expect things to be as they have always been and the failure to adapt as needed when they're not is called normalcy bias.

Let me share a hypothetical situation with you. You're in bed, comfortably sleeping, when a noise wakes you up. I'm not talking about one of those creaking noises that your home makes or the thumps you occasionally hear that remind you to have the furnace checked. I'm talking about that noise that makes you come instantly awake.

You don't want to get out of bed but decide to get up to make sure nothing's there, because, well, someone's got to do it. So, what do you do? You blearily stumble from the bedroom and into the hall. Make a pass through the kitchen and then stick your head into the front room, maybe even stand in the middle, look groggily around and confirm, "Yup, nothing here." Then it's a quick peek in on the kids from their doorway. You saw what you "wanted" to see, which allows you to comfortably return to your warm bed. "Yup, nothing's there," you repeat for your partner as you slide under the covers. All secure.

But if someone really is in your house and in that room with you, do you honestly expect them to stand in the middle of the room and in effect say, "Good job, you caught me"? Of course not. They're hiding in the closet or lying behind the couch, or in the corner of the next room, hoping you don't find them. Luckily for them, you're not going to because of normalcy bias—you were looking for confirmation that everything is fine rather than evidence that things are not.

So it's important to defend against the tendency to lapse into normalcy bias. Fortunately, this is something you'll be able to practice and then mitigate via the exercises in the book.

There is another common bias that people use to explain away events and that is luck.

Why You're Playing Poker and Luck Is Not Necessarily Your Friend

In any potential threat situation, you understand yourself, your motivations and capabilities, and so forth, but you don't know what another person is thinking—nor do you know what they're capable of. Therefore, any situation you find yourself in isn't like a chess match, which is strictly a game of strategy where all the variables are literally on the board. Instead, it's more of a Texas Hold'em poker game. You know your hand, which is comprised of two cards only you can see. You don't know your opponents' two cards. And nobody knows what cards will be revealed by the dealer in the course of play. In poker you make bets based on the odds of any given hand improving. Your bets will also be based on how well you know or don't know your opponents. The same is true when you consider threat situations and personal safety—you know your hand but not the other parties'.

There's another thing you have to factor in: luck. Luck is either a fortunate or unfortunate reality in terms of safety, just as it is in poker. Poker champion Annie Duke explores the subject in fascinating detail in her book *Thinking in Bets*. She notes how people often take credit for good luck and attribute positive outcomes to their skill as well as the turn of a friendly card. They then curse bad luck as going against their otherwise brilliant card playing. The same holds true in other circumstances such as crime or business dealings: Most of us claim good results as part of our masterful strategy and blame poor outcomes on bad luck. But luck is the same on both sides of that equation. It is truly neither good nor bad. It's just random. You can say that good luck brought you and your life partner together for the first time; you can say that bad luck led you to cross paths with an attacker. You may ascribe a good outcome or event to good luck or providence if you wish, but then if you're the hapless victim of a crime, you must apply the same rule. In my experience, people who are willing to do that are like the poor poker player who gets beat on the final card and feels luck was against them. That's simply not the reality of life.

My point here is not to argue providence or good and bad luck. You're welcome to believe in all three, objectively or not. What we can do, with greater certainty, is eliminate as much luck from our equation as possible or, to put it another way, make our luck better. A professional poker player "sees" the odds of filling any particular hand throughout play because they've studied those odds, have added practice to the equation and thus enjoy an advantage over the novice. You can apply your observations to real-life safety and remove as much luck as possible by learning to "see" what is around you with clear eyes and an undistracted mind. It's simply a matter of choice and practice. As Duke says in her book, "The people who learn from experience improve, advance, and (with a little bit of luck) become experts and leaders in their fields." Arguably the most valuable field you participate in is your own personal safety. In the end, luck is an uncontrollable variable that we can't eliminate but must allow for. It just is. Therefore, it's important to stack all other variables you can in your favor.

AWARENESS

Unlike situation, which is largely external to you, awareness is 100 percent within your control. There is nothing and no one else involved in this aspect of your safety. This is not about Intuition but rather your direct objective observations. (Intuition comes after you've become aware of something, whether consciously or subconsciously, and will be discussed in the next chapter.)

Awareness is also dissimilar to situation in that it's an internalized sliding scale that increases or decreases from low to high rather than being derived from our two external situation variables, Safe and Unsafe. Probably the most well-known awareness concept is associated with a colorful character by the name of Colonel Jeff Cooper. Cooper was born in Los Angeles and served as a Marine during World War II and the Korean War. In the seventies he established a shooting school in rural Arizona that came to be known as the Gunsite Academy. He had degrees from Stanford and the University of California, Riverside, and put his academic background to use by penning regular articles on self-defense, but he's mostly remembered for firmly establishing a color code for mental preparedness. It's a good template for assessing your own awareness in any given situation.

White: You are unaware and unprepared.

Yellow: You're relaxed but alert.

Orange: You're alert to some specific threat.

Red: You are in a fight.

In the wake of the 9/11 attacks on America, the US government established a color-coded HSAS, the Homeland Security Advisory System, which in turn was replaced by an NTAS, the National Terrorism Advisory System. God bless our civil servants and their acronyms. HSAS threat levels were color-coded green, blue, yellow, orange, and red. If you have children who were born after 9/11, they've never experienced a condition green or blue, which smacks of a pointless Orwellian imagining regarding daily existence.

HSAS colors morphed into the NTAS system in 2011, with bulletins replacing the color codes. These are presented to you by the wonderfully well-intentioned folks at the National Counterterrorism Center via full-page bulletins that outline America's continuing and generational struggle against terrorism and come in three flavors: Bulletins (for general information), Elevated Alerts (in the event of credible threats), and Imminent Alerts (indicating specific impending attack).

If you want useful information, I don't suggest Googling your government's (if you're American) current threat status, especially through its designated National Terrorism Advisory System page. There is no mention of where the country considers its actual threat level to be on that site, merely generalities about the struggle of good over evil. Out of curiosity I spent thirty minutes canvassing the DHS and NTAS sites and never ascertained anything of value about America's status for November 27, 2019. Unless you consider the federal government's ongoing commitment to thwart evil particularly comforting.

So, not the best preparation from our federal safety leadership, though to be fair, it's a difficult thing to do something like this for an entire nation. In the event of an attack, an NTAS Imminent Alert may contain useful information, but I doubt you'll be rushing to look it up on their website on your laptop or phone. And therein lies the problem with something like a national alert system that has been on an elevated status for two decades: Everyone ignores the warnings, or worse, isn't even aware of them. You've become desensitized to your government's projection of what your security supposedly is. This is true whether you're American, Australian, British, French, or any of the many, many other nations that have a formal threat-level system.

While government warnings are fine if you can find them or care to pay attention, what you need is something more relevant on a personal level. My own awareness follows a pattern of four levels that are simple and serve as reminders to be in the right mindset for any situation. I believe they can do the same for you. Here they are:

Unaware: This is the mental state of disregard for your surroundings, regardless of where you are or what's going on around you. This can happen when you're deep in thought or having an intense conversation; it can also happen when you're distracted by something. Some activities actively induce this state, television being a prime culprit. It's the reason companies willingly pay $5 million for thirty seconds of Super Bowl airtime. If you've ever found yourself on the far end of a lost hour (or two) on the evil that is Mark Zuckerberg's creation, you'll understand this state of unawareness. TV and computers are generally fine though, because you're learning about that all-important, can't-live-without-it, body-toning, new low-calorie beer within the safety of your home or hotel room. However, there is another platform, a device actually, that can steal you from reality, except this one carries grave consequences. No need for a drumroll here, you know it's your cell phone. The most dangerously powerful oblivion-inducing device ever created. Not because of what it is, but because of how you allow it to put you at risk, something we'll explore more later.

Openly Aware: This is best exemplified by driving in traffic or on streets you're comfortable on. When you are Openly Aware you are watching cars, noticing pedestrians, keeping an eye out for potholes or other potential hazards on the road. You're not overly concerned and there isn't anything specific or threatening, but your senses are open to input. Any input. If you're speeding you probably also have an eye on your mirrors, scanning for that lone cop car. When a potential danger does present itself—a pedestrian approaching a crosswalk (staring into their phone screen, no doubt) or perhaps a driver nearing an intersection just a bit too fast—you tap the brake. All of these are Open Awareness inputs and responses. Hiking in nature is another good example. If you can recall a hike you particularly enjoyed, you'll most likely recall the smells, sights, and sounds that were around you. The reason you can remember them is because you were openly receptive to them.

Open Awareness is not a mentally taxing state of mind. You slip in and out of it easily, unconsciously even. And while that's been fine in your life to date, there is power in being more aware of when and, just as importantly, why this particular state of attention changes. Most people should occupy this state of mind for most of their waking lives. Buddhist practitioners and monks seek it at a deeper level. The good news is you need not forgo material possessions or become an ascetic in saffron robes to benefit from this level of awareness. Merely put down your phone and look around.

Attentively Aware: This applies to a situation that demands your attention and is exemplified by driving in heavy traffic on unfamiliar highways, or being in a crowd of people when you're walking along a busy city street and trying to find an address. An easy way to know if you've entered this state is that you automatically turn down your car stereo when you're lost or in heavy traffic as a subconscious means to reduce sensory input. You wouldn't spare your attention or mask visual cues by staring at a phone screen or taking a call in either of these situations.

While Attentively Aware, you are actively searching for indicators and input from your environment. Therefore, it is mentally taxing to maintain this elevated level for extended periods of time. This is the state you should be in in areas of higher risk and vulnerability. For example, pulling a large amount of cash out of your pocket to pay for something in environments populated by strangers, such as convenience stores, movie theaters, or concerts. ATMs and unfamiliar parking lots are also examples.

Think of this level as a natural response, because it has been hardwired into your physiology and biological imperative over millions of years of evolution.

Threat or Thrill: Finally, Threat or Thrill means that you recognize you need to pay attention to what is happening RIGHT NOW, especially in relation to your safety. If you're driving, this is equivalent to slamming the brakes to avoid that pedestrian or the driver who failed to properly yield or see you before switching lanes. Another example would be seeing a hostile person approaching you from a short distance.

This is adrenaline city. As someone who has engaged in high-stakes activities both on and off the battlefield, I can attest that this is the peak of attention to sensory inputs. It need not necessarily be brought on by human threats. When you're playing with your life by BASE-jumping off an 800-foot cliff, you are acutely aware of your environment, though I don't recommend it for readers as a method for comparison. The excitement of many sporting activities or even entertainment events can elevate your awareness to this level.

––––––––––––

Each of these four levels of awareness requires different mental and physical resources. The higher the level, the more taxing it is on your body and mind. Being Openly Aware is not as draining as Threat or Thrill, where your body is flooding itself with the closest thing it has to high-octane jet fuel. Your internal engine can only handle high-stress inputs, even those that are designed to save your life, for so long before it begins to break down and fails to keep your level appropriately elevated. You simply can't sustain a Threat or Thrill level.

This also applies to Attentive Awareness. You can start a long drive paying heightened attention to your circumstances, but you'll eventually begin to lose that keen focus. Recall how a drive like this (or any journey in the greater Los Angeles freeway system, if you've ever had the pleasure of experiencing that) leaves you tired.

Also, it is possible to switch from a state of lower awareness to a higher level quite rapidly. If you're absently watching New England destroy whatever other NFL team happens to be your favorite, and you hear the downstairs window suddenly break, you will not only become instantly alert, your body will also begin fueling itself with adrenaline. Or perhaps you are jolted from a dead sleep in the early morning hours of darkness by the same noise. Your first question will likely be, "What was that?"

What isn't easily done is dropping back down from a high state of awareness to a lower level. It can be challenging to come off an adrenaline surge from a Threat or Thrill scenario. And once you do, the attendant physiological hangover can also make it more difficult to ramp back up, should that become necessary. This is an important thing to understand in the aftermath of an actual attack or one narrowly avoided.

A Few Words on Phones and Earphones

If you're looking to target or commit a crime against someone, the number one indicator that they are currently unaware and open to attack is their being distracted by some kind of technological device. I have done this in third-world countries when targeting known terrorists (who also stare at their phones). The good news here is they are just as susceptible to YouTube as the rest of us.

Unwisely using your phone as a portable television or entertainment device negates everything proposed in this book. If you compound the problem by inserting earbuds and listening to music while you stare at the screen, you are completely deaf as well as blind. How can you hear or see someone approaching you if you've shut off the two most important of your senses?

I don't really expect most people to change their habits or eschew convenient entertainment, but know this: If you're one of the many who choose to be oblivious to their surroundings and the people in them, and remain unaware, YOU ARE A TARGET. You're playing a poker hand blindly to which you are "all in," committed as you are to gambling with the only thing you truly own—your life. If that's something you're comfortable continuing to do, then I wish you good luck with your hand. And also, we should get together and play poker sometime.

If you're guilty of texting behind the wheel, at an intersection or in light traffic (an offense of which I also can be convicted), you should certainly eliminate or reduce that as much as possible. But more to the point, you should reconsider your usage of the device whenever you're out in a public place. I'm referring to that faux "text of global importance" wherein the balance of world power hangs on whether you immediately answer someone about where to go for the weekend next month or just how did that cute cat video get seven million likes? That's the unawareness trap that I see too many people falling into—getting absorbed by the screen anywhere and everywhere and missing the chance to assess your environment.

My appeal to you is simply that you work to become aware of *when* you choose to look at your screen. You would be astounded to know how many times you pick it up and how much time you spend on it. To prove my point, go into the settings on your phone at the end of the day and check your screen time. You may have to dig a bit, but the answer regarding your level of techno dependency will magically be revealed.

What's that number? I'm willing to bet it's expressed in hours and minutes. If not, congratulations, you're in the minority of citizens of the modern age. But again, it's really not *how much* you're staring at your phone screen. Rather, it's a question only you can answer honestly: *Where* are you using it? If you're doing it as you walk to your car in a parking lot at night, or as you walk into your apartment from your car after work, or any of a number of similar situations your daily schedule places you in, you're waiting to be a victim.

BRINGING YOUR SITUATION AND AWARENESS TOGETHER

Combining the external factors of your situation with your level of awareness becomes your state of Situational Awareness, your true picture of *where I am and what's around me, what's going on in my surroundings and my place in them.*

Any place you find yourself can be expressed in terms of your SA by combining your situation (Familiar or Unfamiliar with Safe or Unsafe) with your level of appropriate awareness (Unaware, Openly Aware, Attentively Aware, or Threat/Thrill). For example, if you visit an ATM that you use regularly to withdraw cash inside the office building where you work, it would most likely be a Familiar, Safe, and Openly Aware experience.

Armed with this new perspective, pause here and assess my situation in Mexico before reading further. How would you calculate my SA on top of that mountain before the theft?

To me, the SA calculation during my situation in Mexico looked like this: a Familiar, Safe environment where I was Openly Aware. My assessment was not accurate. Here's how I failed. I'd been in Mexico for weeks at this point, staging out of Ensenada and racing across the Baja peninsula practicing the racecourse, which put me into a familiar frame of mind regarding the area and people. I was comfortable, working as I was—and sometimes arguing—with my race partner, JT, a good friend (weeks cramped in the cockpit of a race car is a great test of friendship). I've known him for years and had, on many occasions, placed my life in his hands. JT had raced in the Baja 1000 series for more than two decades and knew the area backward and forward. On the morning in question, we planned to pack up everything we needed and head for San Diego to complete our preparations for the race, which was to take place nine days later. I had a wicked head cold and was focused on the next several days of final race planning ahead of us, so my observation skills were not quite optimal. Most damning, of course, was leaving $100,000 worth of valuable and highly prized equipment unattended in a country where car theft is a legitimate career path. You can see how mistakes and distractions would begin to pile up under the circumstances that led to the theft (and cost us the opportunity to win a race we'd been prepping for over many months). It was a costly and humbling SA lesson.

Here's another story that demonstrates how to assess SA. At the end, see if your conclusion is the same as mine.

Dhaka, Bangladesh

I drained my third bottle of Aussie Victoria Bitter, set it down on the counter, and picked at the last of the greasy nachos. I was tired after a long day of meetings with US embassy staff and Bangladeshi government officials and was relaxing inside the American Club with a Green Beret friend of mine who was, like me, an American coordinating various security opportunities between the US and Bangladesh. What was unusual for me was that I didn't have any American dignitaries or experts in tow and was therefore free from my usual responsibility of playing host.

The American Club sits on Road 69 in a residential neighborhood in the Gulshan 2 embassy district in the capital. It was one of the places where expats, foreign service officers, spooks, and military members like us could unwind, eat some (relatively) safe food, and talk without keeping our guard up, surrounded as it is by two-stage security and an adequate perimeter fence. It was now nearly midnight, closing time.

"I'm done," I said, dropping a chip. "Let's go. You got the car?" Walking as two Caucasians through the city was frowned upon by the embassy. For that reason, we had cars and drivers assigned to us, locals who knew how to navigate the unbelievable congestion and get out of a jam in the event of an accident. We'd used my buddy's driver to get here.

"Nope. I sent him home. Nothing sucks more than waiting around while other guys drink beer."

A nocturnal stroll it was, then; I had no problem with that. After three years of running exchange programs between the US and Bangladesh, I knew the area well. I hated the city, with its congestion and pollution that put New Delhi's to shame, but I adored the Bangladeshi people, who were resilient, upbeat, and vibrant. We stood up, dropped some taka to cover the bill, and left. As soon as we passed through security and onto the street, I scanned it for threats, noting the few parked cars and ensuring none had drivers behind the wheel or, worse, drivers and additional occupants. There were a few gaps between streetlights and darkened side streets and alleys, nothing serious. With nobody lurking nearby, we stepped off to cover the half mile to our hotels.

It was warm, as it always is in Dhaka, but not oppressive, and at least there wasn't any rain, which can be torrential. Neither of us were armed and we were both quite relaxed after our beers.

We turned onto the main drag at the intersection adjacent to the Russian Embassy, and my companion gestured down a street receding away from us and into a fairly dark distance.

"Have you been to Holey Artisan Bakery down there?"

"No."

"You should check it out. It's one of the few places with some quiet green space. Very popular with the Italians. Great coffee."

"How are the croissants?" I'm not a coffee drinker but have a thing for French pastry.

"Killer."

I made a mental note of the location: side street, not the best lighting, but squarely in the embassy district since there were at least two more consulates nearby. We continued on our way. When we reached the main Gulshan 2 intersection we said our good-byes and I made to turn off.

"You're not at the Westin?" The Westin was the only international chain hotel in the district and towered immediately in front of us, all twenty-four floors.

I shook my head. "I moved my folks to the Lakeshore. Westin's a car bomb waiting to happen someday. You've seen the front." (The building is supported by a column that spans the entranceway.) "One lone truck run up under there and detonated and it's over. Lakeshore's much lower key, plus they throw in free breakfast."

We parted and I walked the few remaining blocks to my hotel, where I arrived safely.

Pause here and ask yourself, What was my SA?

So, what was your calculation for an appropriate SA on my midnight Dhaka stroll? Would you say it was Familiar/Unfamiliar? Safe or Unsafe? And was the appropriate level Openly Aware or Attentively Aware? Hold that thought. Now let me add some final details to conclude the story.

It turned out to be my last trip to Bangladesh, because I'd been selected to stand up and command a top-secret special operations unit, and so I never made it to the bakery.

Sometime later, five terrorists from the Bangladeshi group Jamaat-ul-Mujahideen walked into Holey Artisan and perpetrated the worst attack in Bangladesh's history. Twenty-seven hostages were slaughtered, either by the terrorists or in the ensuing botched rescue attempt, eighteen of them foreign nationals (mostly Italian and Japanese) who were in fact the targets, and another nine Bangladeshis. When they first seized the bakery, the terrorists interrogated each captive; those who could quote from the Koran were either spared or released. A few others, primarily employees, managed to escape by thinking quickly and locking themselves in a side room or fleeing out the top of the building and across nearby rooftops.

Does that change your assessment? Well, that's actually a trick follow-up question because the answer is, it shouldn't. Here's my assessment: The situation was Familiar and Safe, and I was Attentively Aware.

The later terror attack isn't a factor because there wasn't anything in the real situation cuing that conclusion. And while the threat level in a city like Dhaka and a country like Bangladesh is real,[1]

---

1   It would not be the last time I had a brush with a terror incident. Three years later I missed Kenya's worst terrorist assault by a few months when Somali al-Shabaab extremists killed and wounded two hundred people in the Westgate Mall in Nairobi. Those of us from US special ops working in Nairobi recognized it as the target it was, yet still frequented it with a wary eye, and I'd visited Westgate to eat and shop. Were all these people simply in the wrong place at the wrong time? Or did they fail to assess their situation properly and therefore put themselves in danger? What were their options before and during the attack? We will explore those questions extensively in Tool 3, Armed Threats and Active Shooters.

falling victim to hype or distorted perspective is an easy trap to fall into. The Holey Artisan Bakery attack was a terrible tragedy, but also a tragic anomaly; avoiding the city because of that attack would be tantamount to factoring 9/11 into your next visit to New York City. Both situations are such remote possibilities that they shouldn't affect your personal SA assessment any more than America's NTAS bulletins provide any real help in planning your next trip to Las Vegas or across town.

SITUATIONAL AWARENESS EXERCISES

For now, let's return to Rule 1's central purpose. Here are some hypothetical scenarios that allow your brain to understand what a situation looks like in order to build your personal SA. This will create a baseline, the preparational foundation on which everything that happens in a crisis will stand. After running through these hypothetical exercises your brain will come back to what you've rehearsed as an involuntary default setting so that, by repeatedly practicing, you can't help but do what you've rehearsed in a crisis. Think of it as mental muscle memory. It's one of the keys and secrets to special operations success and why we rehearse scenarios over and over.

But before we do, a few additional rules for you to follow. First: Don't be overly serious or somber about it. As you sit with this book or in a restaurant or an office, you are not under a specific threat (at least let's hope not). Quite the opposite. You're opening yourself to a bigger world. One that you never recognized before but that exists all the same. Second: Take someone along with you—a friend or partner perhaps. Two people can observe and gain significantly more than one. If you prefer to do it alone or are traveling, that's okay too. Third: Be confident; trust yourself. You don't need to be an expert to see the world. You've done fine to date. And finally, these are meant to be simple exercises focused only on SA. We'll add more as we incorporate more information and rules, but for now try and stick with the exercises only as they apply to the two aspects of Situation and Awareness.

Exercise 1: Your Dinner with Andre or Andrea

Pick a nice restaurant, not fast food because you're going to be there awhile (as the name implies, fast food doesn't lend itself to spending time in observation, and anyway you deserve a better meal than that as you chart a new and safer view of the world). Once you're seated, ask yourself the following questions:

Is this place Familiar or Unfamiliar?

How many times have you dined here?

Do you know the neighborhood?

Do you think it's Safe inside?

Does anyone exhibit signs of hostility or danger?

Consider the restaurant itself. Really open your eyes to everything. Are the staff professional or sloppy? If you can see the kitchen, how does it look—clean and organized or dirty and haphazard? If you can't see the kitchen, get up and walk around the restaurant and see if you can (be forewarned: Looking at restaurant kitchens with open eyes can heavily influence your order or desire to return).

How about the entrance? Is it well lit? Is it wide enough for multiple people to pass through at once or is it a severe choke point—

if you needed to rush out immediately, would you become jammed with the rest of the sheep?

Is it quiet enough for you to hear if something was happening at a nearby table or in the kitchen or entrance? Or is it a crowded bar where it might take longer for you to recognize a disturbance because you're shouting to be heard?

Use the bathroom. Think about the route you must take to get there. Is it down a long passageway? If so, is that well lit? Is it unisex or single person, so that you need to consider the quality of the door's lock? Could someone attack you there and get out of the restaurant by a back door or other means? Also, how clean is it? Really look, because in my experience restaurant bathrooms tell you much about the quality of the kitchen and whether you should actually eat there.

Less important to safety but indicative of your awareness, how's the décor? When you go to restaurants, do you even notice the art, colors, furnishings? What do they tell you about the place? If it's a chain restaurant you won't learn much, since they're homogeneous, but if it's privately owned you'll garner something, and better still, it adds to your dining experience, or at least it should.

Do you think it's Safe immediately outside? Are the people beyond the doorway bustling along with their day or is it a slower pace? Could someone mask their presence and observe you from among the throngs?

When you leave, is the way back to your car, hotel, or home Safe, or are there places that might concern you or strike you as Unsafe?

You needn't spend a lot of time on all these questions—answer from your gut. Is it Familiar/Unfamiliar, Safe or Unsafe?

Now consider your level of awareness. There might be some cheating involved here. Since you're paying particular attention to the subject, you're probably Attentively Aware, scanning for cues. The better question is: What should your awareness be? Should you truly be Unaware, staring lovingly into the other person's eyes or into your margarita? Probably not. Most likely the appropriate answer is Openly Aware. When you finish paying and leave, I'd like you to have a composite answer in your mind using just the three elements we've discussed. Something like: Familiar, Safe, Openly Aware. This allows you to simplify your assessment into something that's easy to process. And as you'll learn in later chapters, simplicity is key to safety.

Exercise 2: The Streets of San Francisco (or Anywhere Really)

Find a busy street in a city. Someplace that you can walk and where there are people present. I don't want you to seek out someplace that you know is Unsafe, but I do want you out and about somewhere that's new or at least not familiar. Now, go for a fifteen-minute walk. This time we're going to ask questions that you should apply while you're walking. You may also notice that you can transition from Familiar to Unfamiliar within a few blocks or even a single block.

As you walk, are there places you can see or pass that might be riskier or possibly the opposite, particularly safe? Side streets, parks, café entrances, or stores are likely places.

If it's nighttime, how is the lighting? Adequate, or can you identify places that are dark enough that they could hide someone? Or are there places adjacent to poorly lit areas that could hide people, such as low walls or blackened doorways.

If it's daytime, see if you can answer the previous questions by projecting what the location would look like after dark. If you had to pass this way again at midnight, would you? Or is it a daytime-only location?

If you've chosen a major city, be on the lookout for surveillance cameras (London, it so happens, is the most surveilled city on earth, with the possible exception of some cities in China). These will be up on buildings, high enough that they provide unobstructed views, or else on stoplights and light poles. If you spot one, keep looking, as there are likely others, and keep a running tally. Do this simply because it opens your eyes to the fact that you're under observation more than you likely realize, and for that reason alone you're improving your awareness.

What are the people like? Strolling leisurely because it's a sunny Sunday along the Seine in Paris? Walking briskly in Lower Manhattan because no one strolls in that city that never sleeps? Try not to fixate on individuals (something we'll cover in Rule 2, Trust and Use Your Intuition) but rather, take in your surroundings as a whole.

However, if someone does capture your eye because something about them bothers or concerns you, perform a quick assessment using your new skills. What does their walk tell you? Is it fluid and with purpose? Does it come across as ungainly? Are they angry? Is their body language tense, with clenched fists, a set expression on their face? You're not looking to make eye contact here, but as you'll also learn in Rule 2, body language is telling you who they are and what they're about. As important, you might discover that you are projecting your potential as a desirable or undesirable target to others, but for now, simply make note of these people and how they contribute to the situation. Are they adding to its risk? Or do they contribute to the overall safety?

When you're (safely) back in your car, or on the subway, etc., what is your assessment? As in the first exercise, I'd like you to create a composite picture of the three elements, something like: Unfamiliar, Safe, Attentively Aware. It's alright if you have several different assessments for different locations on your walk. In fact, doing so helps your learning curve because it teaches you that these aren't static assessments, but fluid and ever changing as you change locations or conditions around you change.

Exercise 3: The Devil Wears Prada

Shopping is a common situation that can bring you into contact with potentially undesirable humans. Grocery stores are close to your home, making it easier for someone hostile to follow you. Malls and high-value stores like jewelry or even sporting goods stores are also environments conducive to studying your situation and determining SA.

If it's night, ask, as in every nocturnal situation, What's the lighting like? Appropriate? If not, and this is a store you use regularly, look for the best parking space based on distance to the entrance and lighting.

In the store, don't single-mindedly fixate on your shopping list, the clothing rack, or the jewelry display. By all means enjoy your endeavor, but stop now and then, look around. Notice who's around. Anyone in particular who stands out, is dressed inappropriately (whether over- or under-), or is paying attention to you should be noted. Should they be there? It doesn't mean they're a threat, but if you've done the preceding exercises you should be noticing things that stand out by now. It doesn't matter why they stand out, what matters is you're noticing. That's because when one of these things is not like the others, to quote *Sesame Street*, you should stop and consider why that is.

If someone was in your immediate vicinity with the intent to observe what you've purchased or where you're headed, where would they choose to be? It's usually behind you because that's what gives them opportunity to study you for longer periods without attracting your attention.

From inside, consider alternative exits. If the front door was blocked by robbers or the entrance wasn't an option because there's a fire, where's the back exit? These tend to be hidden or marked with "Employees Only" warnings, but in an emergency it's not going to matter, and you should make a habit of noting where they are whenever you enter a store.

While shopping, other basic safety rules should be kept in mind. As you walk out of that jewelry store you don't want to hold your hand out in front of you and exclaim for all to hear, "You shouldn't have!" Flashing new purchases of any kind is tantamount to an invitation.

When you come out of the store, stop, look around, take in your surroundings, whether it's a parking lot with your car in it or merely the exterior of the store. Better still, observe from inside. Who's around?

If your car is parked, observe it from a distance. Use that spot as a natural starting point and then look to the cars on either side of yours. Is anyone in them? If so, what kind of person? Soccer mom in her minivan or Rico Suave in his midlife-crisis Porsche? Expand your view to the next cars. If there's a vehicle with someone who catches your eye, make note of the make, model, and color of their car. You don't need to try and remember plate numbers. But when you get in your own car, look in your mirrors to see if that car leaves when you do or ends up behind you.

When you've completed the exercise using several different stores, make an assessment for each one: Familiar or Unfamiliar, Safe or Unsafe, Openly Aware or Attentively Aware. After you've done that, think about the details (this works best if you actually make notes, if not on paper then your phone's notepad). If or when you return to that store, should you do anything differently? Was your assessment different than what you expected or have experienced in the past?

Exercise 4: A Star Is Born

This scenario amps things up a bit, with greater numbers of people, more sensory input, and more dynamic environments. Next time you go to a movie, play, nightclub, comedy club, or, better yet, a concert, consider these questions:

How's the parking? When the show's over, will it be lit? Lit enough to be able to see into the surrounding cars and ascertain if anyone's watching the crowd for potential targets?

What's the entrance like and the procedures for getting into the venue? Are they constricting choke points or can they facilitate a mass exodus?

Are exits easily identified? Or will you have to search for them in the event you need to leave immediately? Do they add to your safety or is there something problematic about their location, such as being behind a curtain or access to them being blocked by nearby tables or other furnishings?

How's the crowd? What's their collective energy level? Is there abundant alcohol that could serve as collective fuel for violence or frenzied panic (these are almost exclusively the two outcomes for a crowd taken by surprise)?

If a weapon or bomb went off in the distance, how would this crowd react? Would they immediately panic because they're already amped up? Or would there be a momentary stunned silence (this is a great opportunity to exploit, by the way; by being the first to respond, you gain an edge, as you'll learn in later chapters)?

Same with a fight: Would a fistfight spur the crowd to violence, causing an all-out soccer-hooligan brawl? Or would it have the opposite effect, causing a recoil or retreat from the violence?

Let the physical conditions and crowd determine your level of awareness. Can you be Openly Aware, or should you be Attentive? Is the energy such, and your own involvement or enjoyment such, that you might already be at Threat or Thrill? Remember, this doesn't necessarily mean it's bad or dangerous, merely that you're objectively assessing the awareness level you should be experiencing. Keep in mind the mistake I made in Mexico, allowing myself to be less aware than I should have been because of the familiarity, or rather perceived familiarity.

CONCLUSION

You're now noticing details that your mind allowed you to gloss over in the past. Usually this is because those details are familiar or you've become conditioned or desensitized (just like your government warnings). For now, it's merely good that you've noticed them. This is being aware—of yourself, of them, of your surroundings.

I'd like you to think about the exercises you've practiced. You have a new means to understand and simplify your assessment of your surroundings and the appropriate level of awareness you should apply to situations. If you can, as you go about your day and travels, think about categorizing any given situation: Familiar, Safe, Openly Aware; Unfamiliar, Unsafe, Attentively Aware; and so forth.

It may not seem like it at the moment, but you are already rewiring your brain and senses without stressing yourself out. This can be stimulating and even entertaining. SA is a mindset, a set of established attitudes, and obtaining a new one is an iterative process. You need to continue practicing to truly have solid SA. While you practice, know that you're building habits that you will carry with you for the remainder of your life and can also share with those you care about, to make everyone safer in a dynamically changing world. Yet even rock-solid SA is only part of a larger foundation. Next, I'd like to delve into a subject that plumbs a subconscious power so profound it literally speaks to you from the center of your being: Intuition.

RULE TWO

TRUST AND USE YOUR INTUITION

Venice Beach, California

ASHLEY CLOSED THE CAR DOOR, CHECKED TO MAKE SURE HER TOYOTA WAS locked, and walked the short distance to her apartment complex. It was a pleasant late-summer afternoon and she was looking forward to relaxing after a long day at work. The Southern California native, petite at five feet five and with long, light brown hair, had moved to Venice for the oceanfront lifestyle but had settled in a secure complex off the beach because it was a bit cheaper and safer.

The man I'll call Joe Keesling was also a Southern California native. He didn't live in Venice Beach but in nearby Mar Vista, closer to LA. When he saw Ashley approach the apartment complex gate, he dashed up to catch her.

As she entered the security code and unlocked the gate, she sensed someone over her shoulder and a voice announced, "Can you hold the gate? I'm here to meet my friend."

Ashley scanned him briefly. Joe looked okay: late twenties, her age, and a bit taller at five ten, and clean-cut, not your typical problem-type beach drifter. However, she'd lived here for several years and knew almost all the residents and had never seen him before. Then there was his look—not his appearance, but the look he gave her. Creepy. Not quite sinister, but off. He smiled.

Recalling the moment, she says, "I didn't want to be a bitch and thought it would be kind of ridiculous anyway." So, even though she certainly wouldn't want to date a guy like Joe, she let him in. After all, he was here to see a friend. She then walked to her apartment, went inside, and locked the door. She was a diligent locker.

"I went through my normal routine because I live alone. Then I decided I'd do a load of laundry."

She grabbed her basket with a mostly full load and went to the community laundry room on the ground floor. She was busily loading a washer, not thinking about anything in particular. "Then I see him." Joe had stepped inside and closed the door behind him. "I knew in an instant, *This is bad.*"

"Let me out," she stated as she walked toward him.

"You're not fucking leaving," Joe declared and crossed the room, pushing her against a wall and then to the floor. Ashley fought while he began assaulting her, trying to get her undressed. But Ashley was not going willingly, and she fought all the harder, scratching him in the process as she whaled on him and began screaming.

"Help! Somebody help!"

She was loud enough that a handful of neighbors heard through the laundry room window. In moments a few stormed the door, which had no lock, and pulled the would-be rapist off her. In the tussle that ensued in the confined space, Joe Keesling managed to break free, running out of the laundry room and getting away through the front gate as one of the neighbors dialed the police.

Enter Detective Starsky, LAPD.[2] Starsky had several years as a

---

2   A pseudonym. Starsky is married to Hutch, another LAPD detective. As they wish to remain anonymous, I've given them those names purely for the allusion and entertainment value. And besides, who wouldn't want to be Starsky & Hutch?

detective working sex crimes and two decades in law enforcement, all of it with the Los Angeles police. The mother of two possessed a friendly, nurturing, even disarming nature that belied a shrewdness and toughness honed by years of detective work. This nature was particularly handy when interrogating sexual predators, precisely because it played to their perception that she was herself an easy "target" (she's five feet five), something she used to great effect when working confessions. Many convicted felons can attest to these innate abilities.

When she and Ashley sat down, the story poured out. Like most victims or near victims, Ashley unleashed her recollections in a near stream of consciousness. Starsky waited patiently, knowing that not only was this the best way to receive critical information, it was the start of the recovery and healing process. But she was also listening for a clue she expected to hear. When it came, as a single sentence, she noted it along with the other details of the criminal and the act.

"I knew I shouldn't let him in."

"Why?" asked the detective, wanting to hear the reason but not lead her witness.

"Because he was just . . . creepy. And I didn't know him."

Starsky nodded, annotated it in her notepad. Waited.

"I was going to call the apartment manager, but that would be silly. And also, now that I think about it, after I let him in, I knew he watched me go to my apartment."

Starsky had seen this many times. In revealing this information, Ashley allowed the detective to zero in on the single most consistent pre-attack detail she'd discovered in decades of police work: The victim knew what was wrong (the perpetrator and his actions) and knew what was right (don't give him access to you). Yet she acted on neither.

What Ashley "knew" was an inner voice that spoke to her on a primal level. One that's been forged by millions of years of collective evolution yet speaks to each of us individually—"whispers" is perhaps more accurate—on a daily basis. It goes by a single word: Intuition. The lingering question regarding Ashley is why? Why, when that wise and ancient voice called to her, did she miss it or ignore it? That is what we are going to find out.

WHAT IS INTUITION?

I don't want to bore you with Merriam-Webster's rather clinical definition. Instead, this quote makes, if I may say, *intuitive* sense to most people: "There's trouble on the street tonight. I can feel it in my bones. I had a premonition that he should not go alone," from the song "Smuggler's Blues" by former Eagles member Glenn Frey. These opening lyrics provide a great mental image of the essence of Intuition. I have a personal version I've refined over many years: Intuition is a quick and ready insight into someone or something. To me, your Intuition is an unconscious intelligence, one that resides in your subconscious and functions without you actually thinking about it. Ashley knew not to open the gate. She didn't need to reflect on it, her initial reaction told her what she needed to do in an instant.

Intuition plumbs the depths of your subconscious experience automatically and rapidly. These depths are filled with your own experiences compiled throughout your entire life. They are based on patterns you've come to recognize and also outcomes based on events, both good and bad. Remember, Intuition is not used just to avoid disaster or harm. It can also lead you to beneficial outcomes: professional success, making personal progress, and even finding love. Think of someone who entered your life, a person who the instant you met them you just knew was going to be a positive addition. Intuition.

Your Intuition represents the evolution of human consciousness itself, developed over millions of years. It's something most of us go through our lives never thinking about or even knowing exists. Like breathing, it's just there, a necessary byproduct of our existence. This part of your subconscious operates separately from deliberate thought and logical decision-making and even uses different neural wiring and processes.

This is perhaps best explained by the fact that you have two separate mental systems operating inside your brain. They even occupy separate spheres. The first is your limbic, sometimes informally referred to as your "reptilian," system. The limbic is instinctive (more on "instinct" shortly), quick reacting, and entirely subconscious. It has evolved alongside you and every ancestor you've had the good fortune of having in your lineage all the way back to the first one to stroll East Africa's Great Rift Valley. It has been forged through countless generations when reacting meant preventing yourself from becoming someone else's dinner. So, congratulations on your superior ancestry, it's why you're reading this book.

The limbic system is a complex set of subsystems in your brain, comprised of such structures as the hypothalamus, hippocampus, and amygdala, and other words you'll never remember. Here's what's important: It is the source of your Intuition. As Gavin de Becker wrote in his seminal book on Intuition, *The Gift of Fear*, "Intuition connects us to the natural world and to our nature. Freed from the bonds of judgment, married only to perception, it carries us to predictions we will later marvel at." My hope is that in the course of finishing this book you too will marvel at your own abilities.

The second system is called your neocortex and is also comprised of words you won't remember. The neocortex is responsible for your inner "accountant." It operates just as you'd expect an accountant to behave, producing and processing via deliberate and analytical means to deliver reasonable decisions and actions. These two systems, the limbic and the neocortical, do not share well. Depending on the situation, one will exert itself over the other to further your best interest.

Interestingly, you have yet another source of Intuition that resides lower in your body and separate from your limbic "reptilian" system. This one speaks to you literally from the "gut," for the simple reason that it *is* your gut. The human digestive tract contains more than a hundred million neurons, and they are exactly the same as the cells that form your brain's core. So, it would be safe to say these cells are sophisticated and capable. How they specifically assist with digestion, why exactly they should reside there, and how come there are so many is difficult to say.

What is known is that your gut's neurons form their own "brain," functioning just like you'd expect one to, by thinking and sensing, the result being a separate source of Intuition. Because it functions separately and is so powerful, it can cease digestion and send you a warning that literally emanates from your stomach. This is where the phrase "gut feeling" comes from. The phrase itself dates back, in writing at least, to the Hebrew Bible's reference to the center, or gut, of one's body as the origin of our emotions. Your gut is the only organ in your body, besides your brain, to have such a sophisticated personal survival system.

There are some people, particularly within the scientific community, that dismiss Intuition as a fuzzy nonscience without applicable value or provable reliability. Intuition can also suffer from over-masculinity, wherein men feel it's beneath them to attach value to it. Or if they do acknowledge it, it's because they're experiencing a manly "gut instinct" as opposed to the more effeminate "women's intuition," but of course they're one and the same. I can attest not only to its scientific validity but also its real-world applicability, because my Intuition has saved my life, and the times when I've failed to heed my "woman's intuition" I've paid the price. And no one has ever accused me of being unmanly, but that's beside the point.

Let's return to my auto-theft story. That day, after we turned off Mexico Federal Highway 1 toward our speedwing launch point, you may recall I mentioned a handful of small homes. These lined one side of the dirt road, each yard replete with goats and dogs, each a sort of self-contained compound. I was behind the wheel and my friend JT was doing some race coordination on the phone. As we passed the collection of homes, I waved to the few people standing in the yard or sitting on their porches. I can't recall what they looked like, but to this day I can clearly picture their response. To wit, there wasn't one. I'd spent a lot of time in Mexico, and one thing you can say about the people there is they are very friendly.

This lack of response was odd, in a way that bothered me. That's not to say I hadn't met unfriendly Mexicans on previous occasions, but this was different. People hanging out outside their homes on a pleasant sunny Sunday seemingly had no reason to be of the unfriendly variety. I dropped my hand and said something to JT along those lines, though I can't recall what.

A quarter mile up the road, when we rolled to a stop and I'd backed the truck in behind some bushes and killed the engine, I made an uncharacteristic comment.

"I might just hang out here." And I attributed it to the head cold I was experiencing, which was certainly real—I was not operating at 100 percent. But I continued to prep, and we exchanged a couple more comments as we pulled out parachutes and helmets and looked around. However, we couldn't see anyone, and the truck wasn't visible from the highway. Besides, we'd done this before at this very spot. Plus, JT has a way of making adrenaline-fueled activities sound more fun than they actually are. It's one of the reasons he's such great company on BASE jumping adventures. And anyway, we'd be landing next to the truck in fifteen minutes.

"Yeah, I'm in," I concluded, even though I'd made the argument earlier for forgoing the stop altogether and heading straight to the border with all our gear.

We placed our most valuable items in the back seat of the crew cab, under a few miscellaneous gear bags (as though that would stop anyone). I briefly entertained the notion of placing my briefcase with passport and laptop behind some bushes upslope of the truck, but it passed just as quickly.

I told myself if I wasn't feeling up to flying, I could always turn back during the short climb to the summit. This was followed by a rapid succession of rationalizations that I used to dismiss my Intuition: It *was* a beautiful day. Speedwing flying *is* a great time. The air *would* do my cold some good. *Nothing* is gonna happen. I pocketed the truck keys, and up the mountain we went. A dozen minutes later our entire race disappeared in a trail of dust.

One of the reasons I'm angry to this day about the theft of our entire Baja 1000 effort is my complete disregard for two nagging feelings. First, the response from the locals was completely out of character. Second, I'd argued for dispensing with flying and heading straight to the border, where many tasks central to our purpose for being in Mexico (winning a legendary off-road race) awaited. I knew something was slightly off, which is why I'd entertained, however briefly, the thought of stashing my most valuable items in some scrub brush.

But it's the first feeling that's the most revealing. Something was bothering my subconscious about the locals, and I found it noteworthy enough to mention it. What happened in the event is very clear. In retrospect, those individuals told me their intentions. They were transmitting them across the distance between us just as predators have done over eons. When you're planning to do something wrong to another person, you reduce your victim or target to less than human or at least less than yourself. You're not friendly toward those you intend to harm. This form of contempt is a human function and I've seen it plenty in combat.

So what did they do? After we passed, one of them got on their cell phone and rang their local car-theft ring. I'm sure whoever they called was on their speed dial list. And the thieves who showed up scored the jackpot: two gringos and their race car, full-size truck, and all the equipment needed to race. Who knows, maybe they entered the Baja 1000, the bastards. In the end, the responsibility remains ours. While there are many times and circumstances when it's not the victim's fault, in this instance we were two seasoned travelers, one of whom possessed the better part of three decades of clandestine and special operations experience, and we do not fall into that category. No one is to blame but us. And the one thing that could have saved us in the final minutes before we walked up the mountain, that spoke urgently to me in a voice I was deaf to, was Intuition.

THE DIFFERENCE BETWEEN INTUITION AND INSTINCT

It's important to know that Intuition is separate and distinct from instinct, which is behavior that is mediated by reactions below the conscious level. Instinct also resides in the limbic part of your brain and is the activator that probably saved at least a few of your ancestors from the jaws of saber-tooth tigers. I separate the two thusly: Instinct is your automatic fight-or-flee reaction when someone punches you in the face, whereas Intuition is knowing they were going to hit you before they initiated the punch. We're primarily interested in Intuition because it allows you to make decisions and act *before* something bad happens. If your instincts have kicked in, it's too late to avoid the situation and you're simply reacting. Still, it's good to know you have instinct, and we will come back to it in Rule 5.

THE TWO TYPES OF INTUITION

Now that you understand the biological and evolutionary character-istics of your inner voice, let's explore Intuition from the perspective of personal safety. With that goal in mind, there are two types of "action" Intuition. The first is when you're planning to make a de-cision, and the second is when you're under heightened threat. I call these Planning Intuition and Threat Intuition.

Planning Intuition is just what it implies. It is formed by experience and understanding your environment, using your heretofore uncon-scious Situational Awareness. You do this naturally, as a deliberate part of everyday decision-making. Which person should you ask for directions, the doorman in front of the Westin Hotel or the man slumped in the doorway of the building next door? Should I walk down this dark alley or take the longer way around the block to my car? You know what to do in both of those situations.

Threat Intuition is your body and subconscious reacting to inputs received from your immediate surroundings and current situation when they're telling you there's something wrong. That guy stand-ing just too close behind you at the ATM, or the one that's made eye contact one too many times. No matter the situation, Threat Intuition is always (a word I rarely use) telling you two things that are absolutely guaranteed to be true:

1. If it's kicked in, it's in response to something existential.

2. It is without exception in your best interest to pay attention.

Failure to listen to Threat Intuition is the number one reason people fall victim to crime according to law enforcement experts, yet we often either don't listen to it or just push right through despite it, as we learned from Ashley and my own story.

THE ADVANTAGES OF BEING AN AMATEUR

One might think professionals enjoy an advantage over everyone else, but as I conducted research and interviews in the course of writing this book, I reached an unexpected conclusion with regard to listening to and incorporating our Intuition. Quite the opposite is actually the case. Here's another story:

Al Jazeera Desert, Iraq

"Frank Moses" is one of the CIA's top paramilitary officers, with a previous career in one of the most elite military units in the world. And as he explains, even for a professional like himself, turning your Intuition into action can sometimes be so daunting that even the best will disregard their number one life-preservation tool.

"We were conducting nighttime raids in small communities in western Iraq, looking for high-value terrorist targets. This particular night we'd gone in by helo to the first target and cleared it. Then we moved to the second, which was a barricaded building." Not wishing to engage in a gunfight unless necessary, Frank called in airstrikes to destroy the target. His Delta Force team leader was directed by their higher-ups to sweep the building for potential intelligence. "Sunrise was coming, and I stated that the target wasn't completely destroyed and probably had live bad guys given the limited amount of ordnance I'd placed on it. I knew we shouldn't go in and I told him, 'We need to drop another bomb on that.'"

His boss wasn't inclined to wait. In the ensuing debate, Frank relented, and the team moved on the target before it got any lighter and the force lost its best tactical advantage—darkness. Moments later, one of his Delta teammates was shot in the legs by machine-gun fire coming from inside the building, gravely wounding him. Frank called in a pair of DAPs (Direct Action Penetrators, basically heavily armed Black Hawk helicopters) to provide cover for their extraction. Normally Frank would directly control the helicopter strikes, but he was under fire himself and trying to help with the wounded man. Yet, "My intuition told me to take control, was screaming in my head actually. But I had confidence in my pilot, Brad [the lead pilot], a guy I knew well and had used in combat many times. So I by-passed my intuition and said I'm going to let him make the strike uncontrolled."

The first helo rolled in, Brad at the controls, and walked its fire-power onto the target, suppressing some of the enemy fire. When the second DAP rolled in, the pilot either did not have a complete understanding of the target or had inadequate Situational Awareness, because the worst thing that can happen in combat occurred. The second DAP's rounds walked right into the friendly force, instantly killing one soldier and injuring another five. "Two times I overruled my intuition. I voiced them the first time and relented, then let it pass on the second and into someone else's control."

Frank lives with this outcome every day of his life, and the memory is compounded because he literally "knew better." So the question here is, Why didn't he act in either situation?

The reason Frank hesitated even though he twice "knew" something was off was because, as a professional, to halt a complex operation based on a hunch is hard to justify to other professionals. Frank needed to overrule his boss in the first instance. It can be especially difficult to override other experts and people we work with and trust. It is disruptive, and professionals hate disruption. This reinforces a type of loop trap, because there's often no evidence to support your action for the simple reason that...dramatic pause...*nothing happens* when you're right. That was also Frank's second mistake. He had trusted Brad, the pilot, when his Intuition told him what he needed to do was take the active step and control the strikes.

Even for the nonprofessional it is easy to ignore our Intuition because it could disrupt what you are trying to accomplish or, like Ashley, you fear being rude to a stranger at the gate. A silly notion, since Joe Keesling, if innocent, should understand. Yet, like Frank, we don't act on our Intuition. And by "we," I include myself. The question again is why?

It's a very human impulse to avoid disrupting the natural order of things or disrupting others. That impulse can make following Intuition in a potentially threatening situation especially challeng-ing. As Frank's story shows, it can be more so for professionals. Your Intuition may make you disrupt your own routine or goal sometimes, and it may lead you to do things that disrupt other people too. But to err on the side of safety is, well, safe.

In Mexico I had a nagging feeling when my Sunday morning greeting wasn't returned. What I should have done when I noticed it was mentally pause. It wasn't my friend JT's fault that I failed to do so; he hadn't seen it. I should have made it a point. Would that have changed the outcome? Possibly. JT was not likely to be dissuaded, but I might have chosen to stay with the truck. That might have thwarted them, or it might have led to a confrontation. There were four of them, possibly armed, and that calculus can turn out quite differently. And by different I mean badly.

Therein lies the challenge in putting this information to use. You'll never know what didn't happen for the simple reason that nothing did. So how can we ever know if we were close to harm or got away safely? The answer is you can't. But that is precisely why listening to your Intuition is so essential to understand as a foundation for living every day, regardless of whether it might seem silly or unimportant.

With this new perspective in mind, let's return to a location less exotic than the deserts of Iraq or the Baja peninsula—a situation closer to home.

LISTENING TO YOUR INTUITION

Venice Beach, California

Patty closed the door of her Audi and walked to her secure, two-story apartment complex. As she unlocked the gate with her key, a voice announced itself from over her shoulder.

"Can you hold the door?" said Joe Keesling again, ten days after his attempted attack on Ashley.

At five feet seven, Patty could've been Ashley's slightly taller sister. She had the gate open now, was already inside, and turned to face Joe. She didn't need much time to make a decision; her Intuition spoke to her.

"No, I'm sorry. I can't."

"I need you to hold the door. I'm here to see my friend."

"I'm really sorry, I haven't lived here very long. I don't know everybody and I can't."

Patty closed the gate in his face and turned toward her first-floor apartment, leaving Joe on the outside.

"Who do you think you are? Don't be rude."

When she didn't respond or return, he shouted after her, "You fucking bitch!"

Patty, visibly shaken, continued to her apartment. When she got to her door, she saw that Joe was still watching her through the gate. Safely inside, she put her stuff down, locked the door, and exhaled.

She shook off the encounter and after heating up some leftover takeout and watching TV eventually went to bed. She was sound asleep when a noise at her window woke her up. Startled into alertness—which was her survival instinct at work—she pulled back the drapes to shut her window, which faced the outside of the complex at street level, only to find Joe attempting to slide it open. Patty had left it cracked for fresh air in the summer heat. The two were face-to-face and she got a very good look at her would-be rapist as he tried to climb inside.

She screamed as the two struggled at the windowpane. She pushed with all her might against the glass and his hands as they tried to force the window open. And she never gave up. She screamed again, "Get out!" Surprisingly, Joe surrendered and ran away under the streetlights.

She did the correct thing and called the police (something we'll discuss more in Rule 6, The Two Rs). When Detective Starsky showed up, she gave her story and, critically, a good description of Joe. Starsky could now start stringing details together about Joe Keesling: He favored Venice Beach, petite blondes, and secure apartment complexes with apartments that have windows facing the street as points of access (something I will be covering in Tool 1, Preparedness). What was also clear was that Joe's attacks were not drive-by opportunities. Joe had been observing, possibly stalking, both Ashley and Patty because each of them had exterior-facing windows on the ground floor, did not have live-in boyfriends or roommates, and parked on the street, allowing him to follow them or position himself near their gates. Gates are choke points—a location the potential target must pass through—and therefore advantageous for perpetrators. It's analogous to the African watering hole on the Serengeti where prey animals can be found by predators.

But Patty also listened to her Intuition, which probably saved her from being raped even before Joe Keesling attempted to climb through her exterior-facing window, because she denied him access to her from inside the complex. And, of course, she told Starsky what the detective expected to hear.

"Even before he called me a bitch, there was something about him. He made me feel 'creepy.'" What she meant by this statement was actually that she found *him* to be creepy.

Patty's initial encounter with Joe is in keeping with the reason why so many victims override their Intuition when faced with a potentially dangerous situation involving a threat: the desire not to be perceived as rude, which is why Joe Keesling instinctively leveraged perceived rudeness as a ploy to get Patty to let him in after her initial refusal. As Ashley put it, "I didn't want to be a bitch," which is merely a sexist, more derogatory version of the social expectation, especially for women, to be polite to strangers.

Fortunately, Patty listened to her Intuition. Her gut feeling, she explained, was stronger than her desire not to be seen as impolite. She also felt it would be wrong to her neighbors to allow him access. Both instincts come from our social nature as humans, but only one choice is correct for safety. And, I would argue, that one choice is also correct socially. Patty did owe her neighbors social loyalty; she did not owe that same loyalty to a stranger. Furthermore, if Joe Keesling truly did have a friend inside, he would have just called them after she said no. And her misgivings were confirmed when his failed attempt to convince her otherwise escalated into that final hurled insult.

Rudeness and bitchiness. If you are reading this, especially if you're female, those two words are not important and shouldn't even be considered when it comes to your personal safety. Joe Keesling's words and actions were wrong even if you remove his evil intent. Any reasonable person should accept being denied access to a community that is not their own. This too is acceptable collective social behavior.

However, people—and women in particular—do not want to be

perceived as bitches or as being rude. And there is a third perceived social crime women avoid, the notion of being "silly." In my experience none of these are legitimate reasons to put yourself in jeopardy. If your Intuition tells you not to climb into the closed steel box without windows that is an elevator because a man, who's politely holding the door, gives you the creeps, you're not being rude by declining the offer. If he's a good guy, he's not going to mind. Perhaps he'll shrug his shoulders, but he should understand. Even if he thinks of himself as a good guy, he may react negatively, but that doesn't reflect on the woman in the situation. It can be difficult for women who deal with society's judgments, condescension, and the often double standards that accompany them every day. I would never insult women by presuming to fully understand. But I understand this: In the question of social judgment against personal safety, it's important to push past other people's views and reactions when your Intuition is speaking to you. Here's the key: The decision and power are yours. So, if that man in the elevator doesn't understand, should you really care? No. Or at least try not to.

The same goes for walking into the dark of a parking lot when you feel scared or that something, *anything*, is off. It doesn't make you silly to ask for someone you know to walk with you to your car or to wait for someone else. Like the social judgment mentioned above, I'm sure it can be frustrating when you receive condescension or apathy in response, but I encourage you to push past it for the sake of safety. Listen to your inner voice. As Patty did. As Ashley and Frank should have done. As I should have done. This is something I'll emphasize over and over again.

I believe in Intuition's power so strongly, I'd like to incorporate an unconventional and seemingly unrelated source regarding the power of Intuition that has nothing to do with rapists or personal safety. Kelly Turner, PhD, is a Harvard-educated oncology researcher. In her book *Radical Remission* she explores and shares stories from cancer patients who beat the disease by *not* listening to experts. Over the course of a decade she interviewed cancer survivors from around the world who beat the odds precisely because they listened to their Intuition, even when faced with stiff resistance from medical professionals, particularly doctors trained in western medicine. It's a fascinating study.

As she states regarding the early stages of her research, "I remember, on my fiftieth or so interview of these survivors, thinking, *There it is again!*" Intuition ended up "being one of the nine most common factors of Radical Remission among the people I research." Dr. Turner is quick to point out that Intuition does not replace western (or any other) medicine. Merely that there is room and validity for listening to your inner voice, and the effect can be powerful indeed.

What resonated with me was the power of these people's Intuition and their willingness to listen to it precisely because they were facing an existential threat to their very survival. This too can be considered a form of personal safety in my opinion. Perhaps because of the life-threatening nature of the situation, their inner voice—Intuition—could push through the typical resistance we feel when being pressured, whether by our doctors or a stranger, to do something that is not in our best interest. I'm not casting aspersions at the medical profession, and neither is Dr. Turner. Rather, my point is about how you can connect with something so profound it can save your life. That is, if you choose to make the connection and listen.

CONTEMPT AND BODY LANGUAGE

There are two signs that readily assist us in determining the harmful intentions of others, and they are virtually impossible to hide. It may seem at first these might be best categorized as part of your SA, but because they are transmitters of something intangible (intent), I believe they are actually fuel for our Intuition. Contempt, the first sign, is a human emotion. We wear it like a gaudy Las Vegas neon advertisement, and anyone can read the marquee. That's because when we feel contempt for someone or something, we show it on our face in readily drawn lines that advertise "You are less than me. You are not human. And I reject you as a member of the human race." Contempt reveals itself in the way someone looks at you. It's in the eyes. It's in the mouth.

When you are faced with someone who is contemptuous of you, their eyes can appear flat, or "dead," because that's how they see you. Imagine a shark's eyes. But if you can't pick up the cue from their eyes or don't want to make eye contact, the other facial "tell" is the mouth. Contemptuous people sneer. That's because the face of contempt is the only expression that isn't symmetrical. The corner of one side of the mouth will draw back and/or rise, and the more extreme the contempt, the greater the sneer.

Perpetrators trying to win your confidence will often smile to appear disarming. They may do this consciously or unconsciously. Regardless of their psychological calculation, the subconscious reason they do this is to mask contempt. Yet the mouth will tell you, because under heightened conditions, such as coming face-to-face with a victim or preparing to attack, they can't help but sneer. In that moment you'll know not to trust them—and so will your "gut."

There is a difference between passive contempt and active contempt. You've probably personally felt passive contempt when you've encountered images of things or events that you see as distasteful or when dealing with people who you feel have wronged you or your family. If you can conjure the situation or person in your mind that made you feel passive contempt, become aware of what your face does in the instant you think of it or them. You can actually feel it, the tightening of your cheek muscles as they draw back one side of your mouth. For most people it's the right side, the same side as your limbic system.

I'm not referring here to a roguish lopsided grin in the style of Indiana Jones from *Raiders of the Lost Ark*. However, I'd like to point out, there is a scene in the movie, in his first encounter with his long-lost love interest Marion, in which Indy shows contempt and gives away his "less than honorable" nature. He's trying to convince her to do something for him and says to Marion, "Trust me." When he does, both Indy and Harrison Ford, playing the character, sneer. As the expression crosses his face, lit by the evening glow of the roaring fire in the hearth inside Marion's Tibetan bar, we know he's a rake and not to be trusted (until he defeats the Nazis and saves Marion and the ark single-handedly because, well, he's Indy...). It makes you want to shout at the screen, "Don't do it, Marion!" Well, I want to anyway.

In the military we actively dehumanize our enemy as a form of contempt—active contempt. This has probably gone on since humans first began wielding femur bones as weapons. The reason for it is simple—it makes it easier to kill and maim. If you're killing something that is beneath you, subhuman if you prefer, then you're not diminishing your own humanity. Quite the opposite, you're providing a service by extermination. All militaries do this, and it occurs in all wars, sometimes with racist and genocidal consequences. When I was fighting in Somalia against the armed militias there in an attempt to stave off starvation and provide stabilization for the larger populace, my mission was absolutely a humanitarian effort, endorsed by the United Nations and supported by such agencies as the International Committee of the Red Cross and USAID (the foreign aid and development arm of the US government). But when it came to actual combat, our opposition were not people, they were "skinnies" (because of the thin nature of the Somalis). I'd like to say I was immune to this form of mental conditioning, but I wasn't. At least not at first. It made it easier to shoot people. For reasons I cannot easily explain, it didn't hold for me. It might be because I find the Somali people to have a beautiful and fascinating culture. I liked them. It might also have been the region, desolate as it was to almost everyone I fought alongside, but appealing to me because my roots lie in the deserts of the American West.

But I digress. Targeting "skinnies" made it easier to kill them because they were just *that much* removed from human. The mechanism by which that works is placing "us" on a pedestal and the "others" below us—in other words, active contempt. You do not need to experience combat, and I hope that you never do, to see the reason for doing this, because the simple fact is that it's universal and effective.

Criminals who wish to cause you harm or steal your belongings do not see you as a human. This is particularly true of sexual predators, who view their victims (regardless of gender, race, or demographic) as objects to satisfy some missing thing, gratify a psychosis, or gain a temporary sense of power and validation. Joe Keesling's taunt to Patty is both typical and revealing. His disdain and contempt were already there, beneath the surface, and it only took a polite refusal for it to come pouring out in a rage as "You fucking bitch!"

At the extreme end of its manifestation, contempt is the vehicle by which the Cambodian despot Pol Pot slaughtered two million of his fellow countrymen in the late 1970s, nearly a quarter of the entire population, without regard for any real differentiation between individuals. It's how the Nazis convinced an entire nation to commit the most heinous crime in human history against a single and readily identifiable culture through perpetrating the mass extermination that came to be called the Holocaust. Viewed through the lens of history, it's plain to see how effective and even easy it is to introduce the concept of contempt into equations—both passive and active.

———————

The second sign that can feed your Intuition is body language. A person who is intending to harm or rob you will display predatory postures. This is also something they have little control over when attempting to mask intent, because their body is preparing for a heightened "fight or flee" situation. Here are a few of the more easily identifiable physical displays that don't involve studying the face and are not gender specific:

1. Clenched fists

2. Bent arms and shrugged or hunched shoulders

3. Leaning toward you or the target of their intent

4. Tightening of the jaw

5. Prolonged direct eye contact

Recognizing contempt and predatory body language is not difficult. And I've no doubt that in your own life you've encountered them and recognized them for what they are. Subconsciously these indicators (and many others that you pick up on) shape your Intuition. Even when you don't recognize them, your body and subconscious mind will. What is important for you is to know that recognizing these things when they are actually happening in the moment can save your life. Outside of personal safety, they can also reveal much about the state of someone's personal relationship with you. Relationships where one person has and shows contempt for the other are both unhealthy and probably doomed. As you spend more time on your personal safety and practice the exercises in this book, you'll find that it becomes easier with time and iterations and can have great value in other areas of your life. And remember, that asymmetric smile is a dead giveaway.

INTUITION EXERCISES

You might not think that Intuition lends itself to exercises in the manner I outlined in the Situational Awareness chapter, but that isn't true. It's surprisingly easy to tap into your Intuition. Most likely you're merely out of the habit because you don't have to rely on your Intuition on a daily basis to survive long enough to see your next sunrise. However, it can be difficult to set out and deliberately trigger your Intuition, since it usually speaks to us only when needed. It can't, in a practical sense, be generated at will.

The key therefore becomes tapping into it when it presents itself. Start with the following list of impressions and feelings and allow them to serve as indicators that something, anything, is up. (Note that these are not necessarily bad or good but should be viewed in the context in which they occur.) I encourage you to print this list, write it down, or put it on your phone.

Intuition Cues:

1. A hunch about someone or something

2. A gut feeling that something is about to happen

3. Suspicion about someone's intentions or honesty

4. A feeling something is "wrong"

5. Doubt about doing, buying, or agreeing to something

6. Nagging feelings that come to you before or after an event

7. Anxiety. Be sure not to include things that make you anxious as a habit or that you prefer not to do because they're unpleasant. Likewise, if you're a naturally anxious person, don't view that as an indicator. Anxiety in this sense is something that makes you noticeably or acutely more anxious than you might otherwise be.

8. Dark or dismissive humor about something. If you feel there's a joke to be made about something dangerous or risky, listen to it.

9. Hesitation about something or someone

10. Dread

11. A conviction that something or someone is "right" or "good"

12. Knowing you're doing the right thing or in the right relationship, without external validation or possibly even against others' opinions (see *Radical Remission*).

As you encounter these Intuition cues, think about why you're feeling them. Your thoughts may not have any concrete backing, and that's alright. Intuition is, by its very definition, not conducive to quantification or metrics. What I want to do here is restart your connection with your own evolutionary safety switch and inner Cro-Magnon.

Exercise 1: How to Determine Friends and Influence People Assessment

I want you to think of a time when you had a strong impression of someone based only on one (or more) of the cues above. Pick someone who became important to you, disappointed you, or possibly became a problem. What were the first impressions you can recall? If you've chosen someone from your distant past and are struggling to recollect, try someone more recent. Remember, only use very first impressions. The workplace is often a good place to find someone, or while traveling. Write them down. Do it, don't skip this step.

Were those impressions in line with the actual events (disappointment, becoming a problem, etc.)? Do they match that person's personality or intent? Do you feel more confident in your Intuition abilities or do they seem to be off? Spend time on this. Don't treat it as a onetime exercise. Of the three exercises associated with Rule 2, this first is the most informative. Come back to it again and use another person. Earmark this page if necessary and keep the list above handy.

Exercise 2: Planes, Trains, and Automobiles (and the Mall)

This exercise is for when you find yourself in motion or surrounded by others in a public space that has larger numbers of people. Pick from the following environments.

1. Riding on public transportation such as a subway, bus, train, or airport rental/hotel shuttle

2. Walking through shopping centers like a mall, crowded plazas, or public beaches

3. Wandering through the aisles of something a bit smaller, like a Home Depot, Office Depot, or other stand-alone retail center, someplace that will provide the opportunity to observe a broader cross section of society wherever it is that you live or simply happen to find yourself

Now, pick a person, preferably with a trait from the above cues list. Single individuals are better than two or more people. Try and encounter them here and there in the store. Don't get too close—you're not stalking them. And don't overthink it. Just go with the flow. Here are the questions for this exercise:

1. How do they make you feel?

2. Would you ask them for a lift or to jump-start a dead battery in your car?

3. Would you want to engage with this person on a personal or professional matter?

4. Are they a kind person or cruel?

Remember, these are impressions, not calculations nor derived from reason. You're only looking with your gut. When you're not in their vicinity, make a note, not a mental note but an actual note. List what it is about them that makes you feel about them the way you do. Add any word you like to this list, no matter how descriptive or basic. What you write down can even seem off base or nonsensical. That's often the best of all because it's coming from your subconscious and therefore the voice of your ancestors across the millennia.

Think about your answers and these people. Do this several times. Try and come back to this exercise from time to time.

Exercise 3: Mystic Pizza

For this exercise find yourself a pizzeria (or any restaurant), though hotel lobbies will work as well. You can also try a park, but regardless, your location needs to be stationary. Find a lone person again. Someone who will likely remain in one spot long enough for you to spend fifteen to twenty minutes studying them. Don't creep them out by staring. Also, no drinking or mind-altering substances. It dulls your senses. Once you have your person, try and figure out their story. What are they doing there? What does their attire tell you about them? How about their body language? Are they intense? Hunched over? Or leaning back like they own the place?

I don't want to throw a laundry list at you here. The intent is to get you listening to yourself, not some external source or expert (not even me, your trusted narrator on this journey). Because you have more time to consider this person than in Exercise 2, think about who they are:

1. What's their story? Their background and education?

2. How are they dressed? For success, to impress, or something less?

3. What are they radiating? Positive energy, negative? Or are they merely there, occupying space? If the latter, pick another person. You want someone more interesting.

4. Would you date this person?

5. Hire them to babysit your children?

Again, make a written list of their attributes, not just a mental one. Writing things down makes you more aware of them, and the important notes and biggest impressions can then rise to the top of your list. This is where some fun can kick in. If you're with someone else, talk about the person. Try and tell your person's story to each other. As you do, you'll find yourself having to delve into why or why you would or wouldn't start a business with or marry this person. In the end, I want you to reduce them to just a few words, no more than half a dozen. That is who they likely are. Not the details of their life, but how they go about it and the good (or ill) they visit upon others.

Then know that what you're tapping into is on target. Trust it. Believe it.

STRENGTHENING YOUR INTUITION

If you really want to strengthen the power of your Intuition, you'll need to progress past these steps and do more than review the list above (which is not comprehensive, because describing the feelings associated with your Intuition is limited only by your imagination), read this book, do the exercises, and think about it a few times. Taking it to the other end of the spectrum by obsessing over every tiny tingle will likely not produce the desired insight either. I suggest putting the Intuition Cues list and exercise sheets on your phone, somewhere prominent like your home screen where they're readily visible. Look at the cues list from time to time (as opposed to FB, Instagram, and Twitter) so that you become more familiar with it.

Whenever one of these signs consciously comes to you, think of the book's hand symbol and . . . stop.

Think about it in that moment, then go with what that "gut feeling" or "women's intuition" tells you. Later, reflect on how the situation developed and compare your Intuition with the results—which is why writing your impressions down in the moment you experience them is so important. It's only over time and repeated use that you can consciously improve your relationship with Intuition.

Wasatch Mountains, Utah

It was a beautiful spring morning as I climbed a 450-foot cliff toward a BASE jumping launch point known as Echo with a handful of friends. There were a few wind gusts here and there, persistent but intermittent. As we prepared to climb the final pitch (the last 150 feet), we paused. The cliff face directly in front of us had a treacherous and exposed thirty-foot section that once you're past was very dangerous to down-climb. So the spot makes for a natural pause. As we prepared to continue our ascent, I stood still for a moment. The gusts had continued coming and going, not severe enough to force us down, but enough that we were playing a game called "spot the gust." Spot the gust means you attempt to time your jump with a lull in the wind, because the worst thing that can happen to a BASE jumper is to be blown into the cliff you jumped from by a gust you didn't know was coming and slam into it before sliding to your death. There's about a fifteen-second window needed in order to launch, fall, open your parachute, and gain enough distance to be safe on a cliff like this. I've played spot the gust many times.

Suddenly, I had a funny feeling. Now, here it must be stated that funny feelings, anxiety, adrenaline are all companions when you're standing with your toes hanging out, staring 450 feet down into the open space above jagged rocks far below you. These types of conditions are vertigo inducing.

Despite the positive and high energy of the group (BASE jumpers are notoriously high-energy), the good odds of making the jump safely, and my desire to jump, something was pulling at me. It wasn't the conditions, per se, I was intimately familiar with jumping cliffs in the Wasatch, had even built a house at the base of one so I could BASE-jump every morning. And spot the gust is a natural part of the environment. It was something else.

I made the announcement that I'd be down-climbing (not jumping) and concluded with "I'll meet you guys at the truck with a beer." When I turned back, two others went down with me. The remaining two started up the last pitch, then jumped. What happened in the event? Did one of the jumpers have a wall strike and get hurt or die? No. Nothing happened. And that is my point. All of us made it back safely, though two had more fun. Did I regret not jumping? Also no. I was mature enough in my experience to not second-guess myself.

So, I missed that jump because something spoke to me, an intangible impression, difficult to express. I would miss many more and make many more. It was a good call.

There is no surefire method or book (including this one) that can provide a formulaic result you can bank on with regard to Intuition. At least not that I've ever come across. But as someone with a pronounced sense of Intuition myself, I can say confidently that I swear by my own. And you can too.

GOING FORTH WITH CONFIDENCE

My intent with Rule 2 is that you will understand what Intuition is and is not. You will recognize it personally when you are experiencing it and, finally, learn to better use and foster it. Central to this third intent is the message that the more you access, recognize, and then utilize your Intuition, the more valuable it becomes. In this manner it is no different than any other mental skill, muscle, or learned specialization. Incorporating Intuition into your practice of personal safety is a critical component. Is it 100 percent accurate? No. But then, in life, what is? Furthermore, when you're in sync with your Intuition it's damn close.

The alternative is to not rely on your own intuitive input but rather rely exclusively on external factors, including potential perpetrators, to determine the outcome regarding your life (and always remember, politeness is no excuse to dismiss or override your Intuition). No poker player, BASE jumper, spec ops operator, or spy would do that. Neither should you.

And if you're confident, you'll act quicker and more decisively, both of which produce better outcomes (and will be discussed at length in Rule 5, Act Decisively). Intuition, while second to SA as the foundation for personal safety, is arguably the more important of the two. As Dr. Turner states, "I am no longer surprised but thrilled to have been reintroduced to this 'lost' sense of ours, which has the ability to help steer us away from danger and onto the path of recovery."

And now, as we leave the foundations of personal safety that are SA and Intuition for rules that are more action oriented, you should take a sense of confidence with you because you are competent in listening to that critical inner voice. I'm telling you that you are already a natural when it's absolutely necessary, and my assessment is backed by a million years of evolutionary success as well as your own internal personal survival mechanisms. Believe in them, they won't let you down.

PART II

PREPARE

RULE THREE

DETERMINE IF YOU HAVE A PROBLEM

Kuwait City, Kuwait

VICTORIA CLOSED HER CAR DOOR AND ADJUSTED HER SLEEVES TO ENSURE she wasn't showing any skin above her hands, then set off for the nearby souk to do a little shopping in the bazaar on a rare day off. Despite having some much-needed downtime, she was agitated because, as a woman, she had to wear long sleeves and pants in this Islamic country, and it was hot as hell in September at the top end of the Persian Gulf. When she chose to wear more conservative attire in line with local mores, she blended easily into crowds because most people in the emirate mistook her for Lebanese, a convenient mistake on which she'd capitalized on more than one occasion. In reality she owed her Lebanese appearance to her Jewish lineage, which would have endeared her to the locals even less than her American citizenship, had they been aware of either.

Walking the streets of a bustling Muslim city as a lone female isn't a common activity, but Victoria personifies the word "exception." "I grew up in a New York Jewish family that was positively Seinfeldian." At age seven she announced to her grandmother that she wanted to be a veterinarian, which elicited a quick rejoinder that she can quote precisely to this day: "Oh my Gaad, they aren't even real daactahs. And their houses all stink. Can't you find something better?" But that goal was soon to be replaced with a secret desire to become a glamorous Interpol agent because she thought that's who did international crime fighting on behalf of the world's citizens.

She'd always known she wanted to get away from New York and out from under the family. She also knew she was headed for college and didn't intend to attend on her grandparents' terms, even though they'd agreed to pay for her schooling. That's when she discovered the Army's Reserve Officers' Training Corps program, better known by its acronym ROTC. Ever the stellar student, she received a full scholarship to Tulane University in New Orleans and was on her way, but not without a parting observation from her mother. "What are you gonna do in the Ahmy? There's no Jewish boys in the Ahmy." But Victoria, who now had her sights on the FBI, knew the military would allow her to pursue law school, something she'd need if she wanted to become a G-woman. Instead, after four years of Army service, she worked her way into the CIA. Sometime later, after attending The Farm, the agency's intense six-month training course, she found herself working internationally under commercial cover as a spy. The dream job for an escapee New York princess.

Outside her car, the problems began. She'd chosen to go without a headscarf because she was pissed off about having to use one in the heat, and besides, Lebanese women were hit-or-miss on wearing them. But without the scarf she didn't look the part, not enough, because she eschewed makeup and Lebanese women were known for their cosmetic aesthetic—"I wasn't done up enough for a Lebanese woman, and street people could tell the difference."

As she passed a low mud-bricked wall on her way to the market, it started. Several young Kuwaiti men who were hanging out nearby with nothing to do, a common sight in the city, began "tsking" at her. "I'd grown up in New York City and was used to men catcalling, but this wasn't like that. It wasn't 'Hey, baby.' Here it was more like calling a dog, but they didn't want you to come. They just wanted me to know they were there and that they knew I wasn't Lebanese, because Lebanese women get a pass."

She moved on, not rushing. Then she heard them get up and start following her toward the marketplace entrance. Was there a chance the timing was just coincidental? "Sure." But there was no value in assuming that. "It's a false comfort to believe in coincidence." So when she entered the sprawling open-air market, she made a right turn. The group of three men did the same. Two alleys later, she made a left. Same result.[3]

Victoria had a problem. More important, she *knew* she had one. She was targeted because of who she was and how she looked. It was no different than how any potential crime victim is selected. You needn't be a CIA case officer, procuring fissile nuclear material from an arms dealer or disrupting a terrorist organization in a foreign country, to get negative attention. What was important to Victoria as a trained professional is also important to you, and that is this: knowing when you're a target.

How you will ascertain that is the purpose of Rule 3. This is where you apply what you've learned about Situational Awareness and Intuition to assess your situation and determine if there is a real or potential threat. Both SA and Intuition are broad topics, but beginning with this chapter we'll be focusing through the remainder of the rules on when there is a real problem and what you need to do about it.

---

3   A note on groups: Those comprised exclusively of males are more likely to be problematic than mixed-gender groups. All-female groups can be considered benign by default. And you'll never have a problem with groups that are partially comprised of small children.

The first step is to assess your situation, to determine whether there is a threat or at least a potential threat. If there isn't one, it's quite simple: Go about your day or evening. Victoria used a simple surveillance detection route, known as an SDR, to verify she had a problem. We'll learn more about them in a moment, and by the end of this chapter you'll be able to impress your friends with your new clandestine operator skills. Never expected to become a secret agent in the course of reading a book, did you? But before we do that, let's talk about something simian yet also only too human.

PEOPLE, THE SOURCE OF ALL YOUR TROUBLES
(UNLESS YOU'RE A CHIMP)

Humans are violent. Human males more so than females, as the vast majority of battered-spouse cases attest. In some societies male violence is more pronounced, in others less so. Unsurprisingly, violence tends to be a feature of patriarchal societies. In their unfortunately named but otherwise fascinating and insightful book *Demonic Males: Apes and the Origins of Human Violence*, Richard Wrangham and Dale Peterson make the scientific case for why this is so. The authors place humans as a species among the other great apes and note that humans are genetically more similar to chimpanzees than chimpanzees are to gorillas, with tellingly similar consequences for violence. Chimpanzees regularly visit violence upon one another, particularly upon groups outside their own tight-knit structures. Male chimps dominate females mercilessly and target them regularly, but the most extreme violence is reserved for socially external "others." This includes premeditated murder and rape, and waging organized war. Chimps play for keeps, and Wrangham and Peterson conclude that humans are not just an extension of this trait but rather the ultimate practitioners, with our increased cranial capacity and intelligence merely exacerbating the condition, such that when viewed through that Darwinian lens, humans are reduced to "dazed survivors of a continuous, 5-million-year habit of lethal aggression."

Human history is rife with examples of human and especially male violence, particularly as larger concentrations of people view themselves as alike and others as somehow "different." This is the type of dehumanization we discussed earlier that takes place in training soldiers to kill more readily. This is also why in foreign locations or congested cities, targets are typically strangers, readily identifiable by their differences from the locals. However, violence isn't limited to strangers, which goes some way in explaining why so many attacks in the home are committed by familiar, even intimate relations. Seems we're all chimps.

What does this mean for you, aside from avoiding simian society? Simply this: Humans are in fact dangerous. So much so that the likelihood you'll be the victim of some type of violent attack during your lifetime is reserved almost exclusively for human perpetrators (even when factoring in domestic dog bites). And those attacks are almost guaranteed to come from males.

DETERMINING YOU'RE A TARGET

Let's set aside the base human nature to visit violence upon one another for the moment, because even for the purposes of personal safety we should not live as if we are always under threat. This is why having good SA and being in touch with your Intuition are so important. Both inform your understanding of the potential to be at risk and the people in your present environment who might attempt violence or crime. As you've learned in Rules 1 and 2, the key is not to live in paranoia or search for predators or vulnerabilities in every situation or face. Rather, it is to turn to the lessons of Situational

Awareness. What is your situation? And what should your level of awareness be? Just as the Rule 1 exercises demonstrated, let the combination of situation and awareness allow you to see what's really out there. *Then* use your Intuition to give you a better read on the situation and the people in it. The exception is an intuitive reaction to something.

I'd like to reiterate here that the purpose of this book is to instill in you greater confidence in your situational understanding and inherent abilities, to better prepare you for when you've identified potential trouble, so you can actively assess risks and respond to specific threats when they present themselves.

When they do, two types of potential threats will emerge. The first are physical locations or situations that could be threatening: ATMs, dark alleys and parking lots, undesirable neighborhoods, Kuwaiti souks, etc. The second type occurs when you allow your SA to draw your attention to potentially threatening individuals or groups. This is when your Intuition will enter the equation. The exception to this is when your Intuition speaks to you first, telling you what you need to do or not do. In such instances your subconscious has picked up on the environmental clues for you. This can happen quite quickly and is another key to determining whether you have a problem.

Victoria correctly determined she was a target, or at least assumed she was, the two being analogous in her case, by using SA, Intuition, and professional skills. Let's look at a more domestic case for a moment, one where the individual was slower to realize they were in danger.

Canoga Park, California

Hector walked into his neighborhood Shop an' Spend discount grocery and drugstore to pick up a few items for his wife on the way home after a long day. The store was just about to close, so he hustled through his list and stood at the checkout counter, where he'd placed his items on the conveyor belt. The thirty-year-old HR manager was tired, not thinking about anything in particular, when a group of four teenagers entered through the front sliding glass doors. Three were male and one a female, but what stood out was their clothing. Not because it was inappropriate or culturally specific, but because all four were overdressed, wearing coats on a warm Southern California evening. And as soon as they walked past him, they split up and disappeared into the store. He was possessed by a sudden and quite pronounced urge to leave his items on the counter, abandon them right there, and walk out. This was countered by a thought: "Don't be silly or racist." Hector is Hispanic and the teens were not.

"Attention Shop an' Spend customers, the store is now closing. Please make your way to the front of the store, and thank you for shopping at Shop an' Spend," came over the PA system. Hector shook off the ridiculous urge to flee and looked at the clerk and smiled. Beyond the clerk was the only other open checkout line, one lane away. In fact, there were only four employees in the store at closing time: the two checkout clerks, the manager at a nearby service counter, and a shelf stocker in the rear of the store. Around Hector there were three other customers, all queuing up at the two registers. The urge to leave as quickly as possible crossed his mind again but he dismissed it because he was supposed to bring home the groceries. Besides, he'd be leaving in the next minute. He reached for his wallet to pay.

In both Victoria's and Hector's stories, they are correctly reading the situation. In Victoria's case she'd not only identified the potential attackers but assessed the danger. Much of her response was based on training and experience. So let's consider Hector and review the facts surrounding his situation and his assessment as a nonprofessional. Although he wasn't aware of it, he did two things reflexively. His situation was Familiar; he was in his own neighborhood and visited this Shop an' Spend regularly. His awareness mindset as he approached the checkout would best be described as Openly Aware. Even though he was distracted after a long day at the office, he was open to environmental input and therefore he responded to something that was out of the ordinary. He may have been projecting a bias onto the teens, but he was also responding to a discordant cue in his mind, and strongly. And from there his awareness allowed him to notice other, more important details, in particular their coats, which struck him as odd. And it was this clothing discord, not racial bias, that was important. So far so good.

At this point Hector's Intuition kicks in, even going so far as to cause an instinctive fight-or-flee reaction: his sudden and quite pronounced urge to abandon his items on the counter. Intuition rarely strikes with more concise power than a simultaneous physical response and definitive course of action. His response is a beautiful choreography between the two foundation rules—SA and Intuition. However, he pushes his observations (SA) and Intuition to the back of his mind because he doesn't want to appear silly or paranoid. After all, what could happen at a Shop an' Spend?

Your Location and Activity

Where you are and what you are doing in relation to threats is important. Which is why you use your SA to determine potential threats and their likelihood. SA will also tell you what particular type of crime you are watching for. You naturally think of pickpockets if you're at an NFL or NBA game, a FIFA soccer match, or a concert buying food and drink during a break and standing in line with crowds. Withdrawing cash from an ATM on foot at almost any location lends itself to muggers. Darkened or remote locations or separation from a group raise the risk of rapist attack as well as mugging. And in the case of stores or banks, one assumes robbers.

Canoga Park, California

Hector in the Shop an' Spend had his wallet in hand when two of the young men in coats reappeared at the front of the store. Hector looked for the others but couldn't see them. This realization stopped him. The question is, Does Hector have a problem? The answer, because I'm reconstructing the events as a learning tool for your use, is yes. Even though he'd only just realized it consciously, he knew it on a subconscious level because his Intuition had already urged him to drop everything and walk out.

"Everyone get to the back now!" shouted the first teen, and in his hand appeared a pistol that he waved above his head to emphasize his seriousness. The two teens were to one side of Hector, and the exit was in the opposite direction. He could see both his threat and safe haven, and they lay in opposite directions. What should he do about his problem? Before we answer that and continue Hector's story, let's turn to one of the most notorious psychopaths in history for an example of how *not* to determine you have a problem.

TED BUNDY—AMERICAN ASSHOLE

Ted Bundy was a true asshole if ever one existed, and this was *before* he became one of the most notorious murdering rapists of the twentieth century, who deserved to die horribly but unfortunately was merely electrocuted by the nice people of the Florida judicial and penal systems. Before Ted fried, he admitted to thirty murders, but a deductive assessment of crimes in areas he lived in at the time the crimes were committed points to a more likely number of over forty young women and girls. He was born in 1946 and probably killed his first victim at age fourteen, a neighbor girl who was only eight years old and lived on his newspaper route, though he's never been definitively connected with her disappearance and he denied it. His teen criminal record, including burglary (one of his two primary means of killing and kidnapping) and car theft, was expunged at eighteen. His first admitted killing, at age twenty-three, was the murder of two flight attendants sleeping in their apartment in 1969 near Seattle, though he often changed his story because, well, he was a psychopathic asshole. What's clear is that for a decade he rampaged in fits and starts across at least seven states, murdering and mutilating victims, sometimes long after they died when he'd revisit their burial sites and spend time with the corpses.

I'm not interested in Ted's pathology or legacy, beyond the fact that he was an asshole, but rather that his modus operandi was quite sophisticated when he applied himself. In addition to breaking into the homes of women while they slept, his other method was to feign an injury or project some form of helplessness to involve his victim in assisting him (a more complex and sophisticated form of the request that Joe Keesling used on his victims in Venice Beach). This is intended to misdirect your Situational Awareness and blunt or override your Intuition. And it's effective. In Ted's case he'd use it to get women into his vehicle, a nondescript VW Bug, and then immediately bludgeon them to death or into unconsciousness before perpetrating his initial sexual assault. This allowed him to gain control or finish off victims *before* they fully realized they had a problem. As I studied his case, and the stunning number of victims of the repeated kidnap modus operandi, I found myself wondering how many of these women (predominantly between the ages of fifteen and twenty-six) knew they had a problem *before* it was too late.

In the summer of 1974, Bundy moved from the Seattle/Tacoma area, where he'd already killed at least eleven women, to Salt Lake City, where he'd been accepted into the University of Utah's law school. As soon as school began that fall, women began to disappear. In October alone, three Salt Lake City area women went missing, only one of whose bodies was found. This is the story of his next victim.

Salt Lake City, Utah

On November 8 of that year, eighteen-year-old Carol DaRonch, a recent Murray High School graduate and self-professed "extremely shy teen," had driven her brand-new '74 red Camaro to the Fashion Place Mall, a recently opened shopping center in an age when malls were all the rage. It was a drizzly Friday night just before the holidays and already dark at 6:30 p.m. when she parked outside the Sears department store. She hurried indoors to get out of the weather and strolled the main mall, bumping into two of her cousins and a few friends before stopping to window-shop titles through the Walden Books window. She was absorbed in her browsing when a man appeared at her side. He was tall and good-looking with a nice haircut and mustache.

He introduced himself as Officer Roseland of the Murray Police Department and asked her if her license plate number was KAD032. "Yes, that's my license plate number," replied the surprised teen. "We caught someone trying to break into your car," he stated, and then asked her to accompany him outside to see if anything had been taken. At her Camaro she opened the door and confirmed nothing was missing. It was then that she smelled alcohol on his breath and it occurred to her that perhaps something was amiss. "Do you have some kind of ID or something I can see?" He produced a badge from his pocket, and the identification mollified her and solidified his legitimacy as an authority figure. Carol was a reasonable teen and never one to flout rules or get in trouble; she felt it was her duty to comply.

Tucking his badge away, he said, "They've taken him down to the police station. If you could come down and fill out a complaint against him, we have him."

She agreed to go with him and the two walked to his car, the beat-up '68 Volkswagen Beetle, climbed in and drove off. Inside, the car was claustrophobic as the teen compliantly sat in the passenger seat, wedged inches from "Officer Roseland." As soon as they drove off, she knew she'd made a mistake. In other words, Carol DaRonch *finally* recognized she had a problem.

They headed north on Salt Lake Valley's main artery, State Street, until he turned off onto a side street and then again onto a quiet avenue. The increasingly anxious teen began peppering him with questions. As they passed McMillan Elementary School, he swerved to the side of the road with such violence that the car popped up onto the curb with DaRonch frantically asking, "What are you doing? This isn't the police station."

The VW lurched to a halt. That's when Bundy whipped out a set of handcuffs and slapped one over her left wrist. Because she was too late in recognizing she had a problem before allowing herself to be trapped alone in a compact car with a killer, Carol DaRonch's life was about to end.

PROBLEM DETERMINATION EXERCISES

Determining whether you have a problem isn't always easy, especially if you're not sure who the problem is. But there is a special ops and spy tradecraft technique called surveillance detection that can reveal whether or not you're being targeted or followed. Victoria used this skill in detecting surveillance to establish that she had a potential problem in her stroll through the souks of Kuwait City. While clandestine surveillance detection is typically used for more complicated objectives, with the intent not to alert the opposition to your own cognizance, the foundation and basics remain the same. Surveillance detection is accomplished by conducting a surveillance detection route. As with all skills, one becomes better with expert instruction and practice, so while you likely won't be able to build in a twenty-second gap between yourself and a tail in order to accomplish a covert drop or pickup, you will be able to determine the interest of common criminals and predators. Plus, you'll be able to impress your friends with your newfound skills and ability to throw around the term "SDR."

Victoria and I spent a pleasant afternoon swapping tips and war stories on a spring day in a large American city suitable for walking the streets and crowd watching. Listed here are tips to determine tails and also a few techniques to lose them. These are designed for use when walking along large metropolitan streets or in shopping centers where crowds are big enough to make stalkers more difficult to spot.

How to Conduct a Personal SDR

- Stop regularly, look around, high and low as well as left and right. Include stops at random times or locations. Says Victoria, "Be a head bobbler and curious." Stop, fix your shoe, or pretend to. Sit down. This gives you time to mentally breathe and forces anyone following you to stop as well—making them more noticeable.

- Be erratic (changing course where it doesn't make sense or doubling back, for example). This forces stalkers to close the gap so they don't lose you. The more predictable you are, the farther back a tail can remain, making it more difficult for you to identify them.

- Predators, human or chimp, tend to track from behind. When arriving at intersections, don't immediately look in the direction you're headed. First look in the direction you've just come from, then left and right, before turning your attention back to your direction of travel.

- Cross a street. Better still, jaywalk, and if it's a larger street or—best of all—a split street with a center median, your tail will be more exposed.

- Watch for people that catch your eye. If you notice them, make a mental note of something that distinguishes them, to make them easy to remember. Things like "bad comb-over guy" or "should have been a bag lady based on fashion" or "punk kid with too many piercings." If you are moving and see them more than twice, that's a strong indicator.

- A common mistake is to fixate on your destination or anything you're engaged in, like a transaction, particularly ATMs (for obvious reasons). This can be a difficult habit to overcome and even professionals lapse, including me. However, if you're at an ATM and being followed by a criminal, they almost certainly will keep you under observation, and by merely looking around, you can "out" your tail.

- When seated indoors or walking where windows are part of your landscape, use both windows and mirrors to see what's around. Mirrors are particularly helpful in restaurants where they're used to create the illusion of greater space or a more open environment, and you should always notice them. The more you practice window "washing" (cleaning scum from your view), the better you'll become. Using windowpanes angled at 90 degrees to each other and that allow you to see at angles works particularly well. Also, two windows, or a window and a mirror, that face each other provide a cunning means to look in the direction you expect to see someone approaching from when you don't want to be looking directly at them (the mirror or window into which you're peering will be offset from the final, third angle and therefore it won't appear that you're looking directly at the person). Selecting restaurants with mirrors is a common clandestine trick. Choosing your seat and spot in a restaurant or where to stop on the street becomes an art in and of itself. The old adage of never having your back to an entrance or window isn't, therefore, always the law. You may choose a vantage point that puts your back to entrances. If you want to be "spy tricky," use your wine glass or other glass objects—even ones on your neighbor's table can sometimes be of use, though minimally—to see behind you. The windows-and-mirrors game is fun to experiment with, and I encourage you to make a habit of it.

Means to Lose or Counter a Creeper When You've Got One

- In stores or restaurants, approach an employee and tell them, "There's a creep following me. Can I use your back door to lose them?" If it's a lone creeper and you're female, visit a female-centric store if possible. Baby Gaps and Victoria's Secrets work well. A lone male, especially one that's following you for nefarious purposes, will not only stand out but be uncomfortable. That alone will buy you breathing space and change a "hasty" situation to a "deliberate" one, a desirable transition (see next chapter, "Develop a Plan").

- If in an area with an escalator, take it. Up is best because it gives you the high ground for observation, but either way it forces a pursuer into a long and confined channel that you can easily observe. Another tactic is to go up, then straight down. If you cross, you'll be able to get a much better view of them. Avoid elevators to change floors. Stairs work almost as well except when doubling back, as you'd be face-to-face without the benefit of a barrier.

- This brings up the subject of eye contact. If you think they're trying to make you a target, letting them know you know they're there is a good countermeasure. A direct look in the eye is better than a furtive glance over a shoulder, because that is displaying prey animal behavior and you want them to know you're a predator too. "It's always an iffy proposition," says Victoria. "If they're trying to be sneaky, eye contact can work because they'll be surprised. But you don't want to encourage them." My recommendation is if you make eye contact and if something passes between you and the creep, accompany your look with a nonverbal gesture making clear your intention and awareness. A shake of the head or "no no" finger gesture works well.

- I don't recommend verbal contact or confrontations and certainly not in poorly lit or isolated locations. However, if you're pushed into a face-to-face beyond your control, use a direct "Stop following me" or "Did you need something?" Also, dialing your phone and getting anyone while pretending it's your husband, wife, boyfriend, bodyguard, whatever and saying into the phone as they pick up, "There's a creep here bothering me," is perfect. Calling the police in front of him is even better. As soon as the operator answers with "9-1-1, what's your emergency?" simply tell them, "There's a man following me and he's right here, I'm at _____." He'll get that message without ambiguity. And if he calls you a bitch? Just smile. Better that than a creeping son-of-a-bitch stalker.

- Footwear is an important consideration, especially for females. Victoria has a strong opinion and remedy if you're a member of the Jimmy Choo shoe crew. As with phones, she explained to me, "You will never be able to tell a woman not to wear her 'hot' shoes. It'll never happen, but they're a big differentiator in escaping. The solution is to take them off. Because bare feet are better than stilettos." In almost any situation, including big cities, short of Chicago in January, you're better off barefoot when you need to "beat feet."

- Places to be avoided both for conducting an SDR and as a lone individual are parking structure stairwells, and restrooms down long corridors (such as in shopping malls) or in poorly lit environments. And dead ends are right out.

CONCLUSION

There are an infinite number of variables and situations, and therefore it's impossible to demonstrate them all. But don't let that bother you. Putting it all together in determining whether you have a problem or not isn't a complex or time-consuming matter. In all three stories above—Victoria in Kuwait, Hector at the Shop an' Spend, and Carol DaRonch in Salt Lake City—each person arrives at one of two conclusions, whether consciously or unconsciously: Either they have a problem, or they do not. It's a binary either/or decision. All three arrived at their decision at different points in their respective journeys. As expected, Victoria, a professional CIA case officer, correctly assessed her situation long before it became an existential threat. What is important for you is to use your Situational Awareness and Intuition to guide you when you are faced with a potential threat so that you can make the right decision before, like Carol and possibly Hector, it's too late to take action to avoid a life-threatening situation.

Remember, you can do everything correctly and still be targeted. Furthermore, it should be clear by this point that you are already equipped with the tools and instincts needed to determine if you are a target. Millions of years of evolution and survival have gone into your preparation, and you should be confident in your abilities. Everything you've read to this point has been designed to arrive at that decision and it needn't be involved or complex. Just the opposite. It should be a rapid and simple conclusion. Everything that follows in this book is designed to help you after you've made the decision that you have a problem but before you can say, "I've just climbed into a car with Ted Bundy."

RULE FOUR

DEVELOP A PLAN

Kuwait City, Kuwait

VICTORIA KNEW SHE HAD A PROBLEM WITH THE THREE MEN TRAILING her into the bazaar, which was just far enough away to raise her level of concern. Things would not go well if she allowed herself to become isolated or worse, kidnapped. She needed a plan. And she needed to develop this plan on the fly—stopping to think about it wasn't an option since she was already being targeted. Falling back on her training, Victoria focused immediately on the desired end state. She needed to either lose them or discourage them enough that they lost interest and wandered away on their own. So her plan began with that end in mind. With that clarity, she could figure out what she needed to do to safely resolve her problem. And that's exactly what you should do as well.

YOU GOTTA LOVE IT WHEN A PLAN COMES TOGETHER
(HOW TO BUILD YOURS)

Developing a plan is similar to Situational Awareness; it's best broken down into parts that are logical and simple to use or recall even under duress. And like SA, thinking and learning about planning provides a foundation that, when coupled with practice, makes for a much more sure poker bet. Because, as with everything contained in this book, the outcome is more certain the better prepared and rehearsed you are.

Beginning with the end, how do you want your story to end? That the third act and climax of a story is important is no secret in Hollywood. And so it is with your personal safety. From the end you'll be able to determine the steps needed to arrive safely, just like the hero of your own personal movie. Roll credits and plan the blockbuster sequel.

Personally, once I've established my desired end state, I make one more simple and rapid determination. Is my plan a deliberate or hasty one? This is an important decision to make quickly because it is determined by how much or little time you have.

Deliberate planning: In this case you're not pressed to make a decision but can consider your options as well as the steps needed to arrive safely at your end state. For instance, if you've established that someone's followed you to a restaurant where you're having dinner (thanks to your newly acquired SDR skills) and you think they may be waiting for you to leave, you have time available to make a plan. Another form of deliberate planning is to make your plan beforehand. If you're going to be traveling through a higher-risk neighborhood or city, you can build a plan to mitigate threats.

Hasty planning: Here you have little to zero significant time to work out what you need to do. Victoria being tailed by street thugs in the souk needs to make a hasty plan. Even if someone is threatening to attack you or someone else nearby, you should still plan before acting if at all possible.

There are of course times when planning is imprudent or simply not possible. Those instances will be discussed at length in Rule 5

(Act Decisively). For now, let's cut straight to the final climactic scene of your personal movie by visualizing how the story ends.

BEGINNING WITH THE END IN MIND

What is the outcome you want? Ask yourself questions: If I'm separated from my car by the threat, as Victoria is, what do I need to do? Must I get to my car right now? If so, do I need help to do it? Or can I use different transportation to get away and come back later? Should I stay put and get help to come to me? If someone is following me on the street, do I need to get back to my home/hotel or will another place suffice? Can I get away on my own? Is there an immediate trustworthy person I can contact or whose attention I can attract?

Regardless of what the many variables are, select an end state and then stick with it. This choice allows you to develop a plan, and having one is what will save you if things continue to evolve in a negative way or if you feel like you don't entirely understand the situation because you don't know all the variables. So, try and picture that end state (the car, hotel lobby, or safe crowd) and then put the image squarely in your mind.

No matter the situation, once you know what the end state is, work backward from there. Ask the questions that make sense to you. You needn't be an expert in cloak-and-dagger tactics to know that being in a restaurant or public facility with people in it will mitigate the immediate threat or that a parking lot attendant could help in a car-related situation. Immediate safety now (something temporary or nearby) is more important than final safety. If it provides a respite, take it. From there you can develop a better or perhaps more complete deliberate plan, but the important thing is to remove the immediate threat. Don't be afraid to throw off your schedule or to disrupt someone else's day. As we've determined, it's not silly to listen to your Intuition. And it's never silly or foolish to interrupt another person because you think they can help. On the contrary, to do so is to show true wisdom.

So, with the end in mind you can begin the process of developing your hasty or deliberate plan.

Deliberate Plans

Deliberate plans are really only differentiated by the fact that you have time, either in the course of your activities or beforehand. That difference is significant insofar as you're not under immediate pressure and are therefore less likely to make matters worse or make a mistake. Making a deliberate plan needn't necessarily be in response to an existential threat. Prudence is a completely acceptable justification, as the following story by Dutch, the former operator at my top-secret unit, demonstrates. We were running low-visibility operations to defeat a specific terrorist threat in the region, and I'd deployed him as a member of a joint special operations team.

A Middle Eastern City

The barbershop was closed. It was a few minutes after eight a.m., and Eli, Dutch's interpreter, said that it should have opened already. Dutch backed away from the door and glanced down the sidewalk to his left and right. Eli cupped his face to the glass, trying to see deeper into the small dark room for signs of movement. Other shops along the street were beginning to open, and trucks were stopping in the road and making their deliveries. Dutch quickly debated whether or not they should get back in the car and do a short ten-minute

SDR out and back to determine if anyone was following or showing interest in them, or continue to wait out front. His plan that morning had already included one SDR on their way to the barber. Normally he wouldn't be too concerned about waiting a few minutes, since he traveled regularly to stores and businesses throughout the city, but once seated in the barber's chair he would be more vulnerable than sitting at a restaurant with two or three armed teammates. And no one from his team had used this barber before, so he was being more cautious than usual due to the increasing threats they were facing from Al Qaeda.

In late September 2012, the city was beginning to crack. Just a couple weeks earlier, the American Embassy had been attacked, causing significant damage to the compound and destroying many vehicles. Dutch's team, who lived across town in their own house, prepared for the worst but continued to live and operate with little to no terrorist interference. Unlike most of the Americans in the city, who were locked down in either the US Embassy or the Sheraton Hotel, the team enjoyed relative freedom going wherever, whenever they pleased. The city was also riddled with various criminal networks, and the team never underestimated the threat these posed since it was their job to seek them out.

Because Dutch's team was self-sustaining, they were responsible for maintaining vehicles, housing, groceries, cooking, security and so forth, so they were always busy. But not today. Today was kind of a day off, meaning that they weren't running any ops. Dutch hadn't had a haircut in months and felt the need to get cleaned up. Due to his specialty he seldom had a reason for official engagements and was usually on the streets, where a scruffy appearance was beneficial for a white guy trying to keep a low profile. Unfortunately, the barber he'd always used in the past had closed. The business he found himself in front of had been recommended by Eli, a tall, bald, gregarious guy of unknown origin. They got along well.

Normally, Dutch and his teammates traveled in buddy teams for security. However, not today. For that reason he'd made a more deliberate plan to cross the city and visit the unfamiliar business. This was also the first time he was out alone with Eli. Not a big deal, but it meant he was the only one who was armed, carrying a Glock 19 in a slim holster shoved down the front of his pants. An uncomfortable position at first, but after a while you got used to it. Having the gun in front kept it more concealed, no bulge on the hip and therefore less likely to be seen by the casual observer. This also made it easier to draw from a seated position. His left front pants pocket held a spare magazine and a Benchmade tactical knife. The right front pocket held a cell phone, and in his messenger bag was a concealed H&K MP7 machine gun. All of these devices were a means to support his contingency plan in the event of an attempted kidnapping, an ever-present threat in a city that valued individual Americans as hostages or trophies.

Still, hanging out on the street as a white guy wasn't a good idea, even on a sleepy morning. Just as he was getting ready to tell Eli to get back into the car, the interpreter spotted the barber walking in their direction. "That's him, he's here." He and Eli greeted each other in Arabic and shook hands. The barber had fled Iraq a few years before. How he ended up in this new country, Dutch couldn't remember, but he and Eli had known each other for a while. As the barber unlocked his front door, Dutch did a quick 360, making a mental note of the foot traffic on the street, looking for anything "out of the ordinary" before stepping inside.

It was dark. Evidently the barbershop didn't have power. The barber disappeared into a small back room for a few minutes before emerging with a generator that he pushed on a fabricated cart along with several extension cords. As the American looked out the window, Eli helped the barber steer the generator through the narrow door and onto the sidewalk, where they chained and locked it to an iron ring that had been set in concrete (snatch-and-run crime was rampant). A few minutes later, the barbershop flickered to life. The TV was tuned to a soccer game, Arabic music played from an ancient radio. In short order, Dutch was seated and telling Eli, who translated to the barber, how he would like his hair and beard trimmed, not that it really mattered. Dutch was pretty sure the barber was going to cut it how he thought it would look best, which is exactly what he did.

As soon as the barber threw the cape over him and turned to grab his comb and scissors, the American drew the Glock and placed it under his left thigh. It was the same placement he used when serving as the driver on outings, because it allowed him quick access with his shooting hand while keeping the weapon secured. In the event he encountered a threat while stopped in traffic he could quickly engage anyone on his side or in front of the vehicle with a subtle movement. A small detail, to be sure, but planning wasn't something that stopped as soon as you were stationary.

Through the mirror on the opposite wall, Dutch observed the foot traffic outside the window.[4] There was no way he'd allow himself, out alone, to be seated where he couldn't watch the entrance, knowing that even a few seconds' advance notice could make all the difference. The running generator, crackling radio, and boisterous conversation between Eli and the barber drowned out the sounds of the city street. For the better part of an hour and a half, the Iraqi meticulously trimmed, shaved, and treated his scalp. "It was amazing. I have never in my life had such a fantastic service experience. I told him if he could get to the States, men would pay a hundred dollars a head or more. He charged me twenty dollars, I gave him fifty," he recalls. Though he was relaxed, in his mind he still walked

---

4   Notice how he uses mirrors to improve his SA.

through primary and alternate contingency plans, one for standing his ground, the other for escape.

His memory of the haircut remains a pleasant and benign experience. He and Eli left without incident, stopping to grab some shawarmas on the way home for the rest of the team.

Two months later Dutch left the country for good, never to return. During that time he made two more visits to the same barber. Each experience as good as the first, if not better. Each time trying to enjoy the experience as much as possible while still remaining vigilant. And each visit required three plans: before departing the safe house, during the haircut, and for the return trip.

"I'd been back home for about a month when I heard the news. Three members of AQ [Al Qaeda] had attempted to kidnap one of my replacements while he was getting his haircut at my barber. They burst through the door of the barbershop armed with pistols and a stun gun. The American shot and killed two, wounding a third who escaped. I was always mentally prepared for this to happen whether at a barbershop, restaurant, or stuck in traffic. We practiced the art of planning our activities, being vigilant, prepared, and keenly in command of our surroundings. This allowed us to always keep two or three steps ahead of 'what could happen.'"

———————————

The takeaway from Dutch's story is not the exotic location, high threats, or his alertness level but that along every step of his barber excursion he had a plan. Dutch did everything right, planned his route in advance, used SDRs, practiced good tradecraft (maintained SA), and continued to think about what the likely threats at his destination were and how to contend with them. The later kidnappers were only thwarted because in the end their intended victim was better prepared than they were. Dutch's time in-country highlights the fundamentals and challenges in personal security planning when you're in an environment where the potential for attack exists. And this country in 2012 was certainly such a place. But you needn't be facing Al Qaeda on the Arabian Peninsula to deliberately plan like this. I've done the same thing as Dutch in Bangkok and New York.

Las Vegas, Nevada

I was in town on business and the legendary Alan Parsons Project was playing a Saturday show, and since I happen to be friends with some of the band I got invited to the concert. It was Super Bowl weekend 2020, and after a brilliant show they were staying in town to watch the game and kindly included me on their VIP list. I stayed an extra night because, well, who wouldn't want to watch the Super Bowl with the Alan Parsons Project?

The game was projected on probably two dozen giant screens throughout the hotel's banquet hall, which was filled with at least a thousand people. The band had two reserved tables in one corner, and we'd all settled in for drinks and free food, including Alan and his wife, Lisa, to enjoy the game. I was sitting with my good buddy Dan Tracey—one of their two guitarists—along with bassist Guy Erez, lead guitarist Jeff Kollman, and lead singer P. J. Olsson. All of these guys were bona fide rock stars, making me the odd man out. At an adjacent table in our corner of the banquet hall were four nice local couples and two guys I'm going to call Bruce Lee Junior and Sleeve Tattoo.

Now, Bruce and Sleeve were clearly drinking heartily and probably railing coke, because they would disappear to the bathroom regularly and come back with intensity simply radiating off them. In the second quarter, with Kansas City and San Francisco tied, the crowd was riveted to the game. Bruce kept standing up and blocking the view of Guy, who got his attention and politely asked, "Would you mind sitting down, I can't see. Thanks." Guy is very easygoing with a penchant for psychology and not easily riled.

Bruce Lee Junior, considering this request with all the patience of an eight ball of cocaine, responded with, "You want to fucking take this outside?" and began baiting first Guy and then Dan Tracey, who I have to add is autodialed to any affront to his bandmates and, as opposed to laidback Guy, did not suffer fools. The exchange escalated between Bruce Lee and primarily Dan, who, I realized, was ready to throw down in the event Bruce attempted a swing (he was making these subtle martial arts moves, thus the nickname). I'd add here that the band would have cleaned these two clowns' clocks without any help from me. Instead, I focused my attention on whether Bruce and Sleeve had any more friends and kept a wary eye on the proceedings, hoping security would show up so it wouldn't get out of hand. Bruce kept repeating, "You want to take this outside? Let's go outside," to Dan, Guy, Jeff, and me. He even kept taking steps toward the exit, only to return again just as intense when no one would follow. It was an unfortunate situation and more of a distraction than a real threat. Until.

Bruce was on a coke upswing, and in a moment of Napoleonic (he was a short little guy) fury as he stood above the still-seated Guy (who was smart enough not to stand and fuel the escalation) declared, "I've got a .45 in my car and I'll fucking shoot you."

At this point you may think that the situation was calling for us to act (Rule 5) or formulate a hasty plan (which we'll get to next), but that's not the case. I immediately went into deliberate planning. First, I actually got Bruce's attention and said, "You don't want to say that," which was probably a ridiculous thing to say since you can't reason with or calm someone on a coke binge or who's pushing for a confrontation. For my effort I got a "Fuck you. Let's go." Dan Tracey also jumped in and the arguing continued, with Bruce still keen to take things outside.

But I knew we had time because if Bruce was serious and/or had his gun, he would have pulled it out and brandished it at that point. So even though the situation was tense, time was on my side and I used it to formulate two options, neither of which included going outside or attempting further discussions with Bruce. Even though blows could be exchanged without much warning, the real threat, the gun, was not part of the situation. Yet.

First, I began with the end in mind. What did I want? I wanted us (the band, innocent bystanders, and me) to be safe. Second to that, I wanted to de-escalate the fight and for everyone to get back to enjoying the game. Personally, I felt a strong sense of responsibility because Alan is this very polite and gentle giant of a Scotsman and if a fight broke out while I was there as a guest, I'd feel culpable regardless of who initiated it. Also, Dan kept mentioning to Bruce Lee in reference to me that "You don't want to mess with this guy," and "You don't know who you're messing with." While both statements were true, it kept fueling Bruce who, hopped up on Columbia's finest, wouldn't have known who he was dealing with even if it'd been Chuck Norris.

Furthermore, the reason why Bruce and Sleeve didn't want to mess with me wasn't my ability to channel my inner Chuck Norris, it was something criminals like them could never foresee or comprehend. I was deadlier than they could conceive because I knew how to plan in a crisis.

If Bruce wouldn't drop the matter (still a hopeful if remote possibility), my deliberate plan was I'd either agree to go with him or follow him as he went out to collect his gun. On the walk through the banquet hall (it was quite long) I'd scan for and then identify casino security and get their attention. Failing that, at the hall entrance there was a screening point and I could find someone there. At that point I'd turn it over to security, and if Bruce made a run for it, only then would I engage physically. There was no way I was going to let him out of my sight outside after his threat. I'd also be forced to bring in the police and press full charges for the same reason. Kicking him out would only enrage him, and so to jail he'd need to go.

My alternative deliberate plan, if Bruce didn't get any takers, would be to watch him closely. (I couldn't be sure that the two guitarists wouldn't take him up on his offer to go outside. One thing I'll say about real rock and rollers like these guys, as opposed to some of the posers I've encountered, is that they're not afraid to throw down.) If Bruce got up suddenly and left with speed and purpose, I'd need to reposition myself so I could watch from behind my seat when he returned. It was now completely feasible that Bruce (who'd by now told us he'd been in jail for assault multiple times because he was such a badass) would return with his .45 and shoot one or all of us. I began my mental checklist on how to deal with a potential active shooter like Bruce.[5]

I didn't share these plans with my rock and roll buddies. What's important is I'd deliberately planned for and was ready for either scenario. The question then became what would Bruce do? Because sometimes, as Alan Parsons's fellow Scotsman, their national poet Robert Burns, wrote, even the best-laid schemes o' mice an' men go oft awry. And Bruce could upend my plan simply by doing something radically different than I could imagine. So, when your best-laid plans don't work and you find yourself in a potential crisis, you may be left with no choice but to make a new plan. One that doesn't allow for much time—in other words, a hasty plan.

Hasty Plans

A hasty plan should be just that, hasty. It shouldn't take much time by its very definition since, well, you don't have deliberate time

---

5   This is something I will talk about how to deal with explicitly in Tool 3, Armed Threats and Active Shooters.

available. As with all personal safety plans when you're faced with a threat, begin with the end in mind. Only now, facing a real threat, the pressure is on, and strange as it may sound, it's time for a kiss.

Kiss, or KISS, is an acronym that really means finding the simplest and fewest steps in any effort to arrive at your goal. It's usually associated with the military because, where I came from, we like everything as basic as possible. The term's originator was a man named Kelly Johnson who designed and built the SR-71 and U-2 spy planes, for decades the fastest and highest-flying aircraft in the world, and was a guy who knew something about how to make the complex simple to reduce risk. His motto was, "Keep it simple stupid—KISS—is our constant reminder."

Like military planning, simplicity should be ever in your mind. The following stories demonstrate simple plans and reveal how the plans we either make or don't can make all the difference.

Kuwait City, Kuwait

Victoria's rapid plan and desired end state were to either lose her three Kuwaiti stalkers or discourage them from further pursuit. As she walked, she began taking stock of relevant details about her environment. First, there was some daylight left so darkness was not a concern. Also, if she kept walking toward her destination she'd encounter more people, and there is safety in numbers (as the cliché goes). Even if they're locals who may not be disposed to offer immediate help, large crowds going about their daily lives are a good thing.

The entrance to the souk was a narrow alleyway, but beyond that she saw the crowds, and they became her first step. Behind her she could hear the pursuers. They were speaking Arabic (which she does not), so she wasn't sure if they were talking about her, but they were closing the gap. Because she didn't want a confrontation, she stayed focused on her plan. Inside the bazaar she calculated her next step. She needed more than just numbers of people, she needed faces she might be able to trust. As she wound her way through the Arabic crowd she kept an eye out for anyone who might look like her, because even if she lost her pursuers in the souk, they merely needed to wait for her to return to her car if they were determined to target her. In Victoria's case, she was scanning for non-Kuwaiti faces, and any foreigner, preferably several, would do. In the masses she spotted them, two twentysomething males, and she had little doubt that they were American soldiers. "I could tell they were military because they all walk the same."

Without bothering to look behind at her pursuers, she made straight for the two soldiers and introduced herself. "I told them I had three guys following me and asked if they'd walk me to my car." Victoria's plan was simple and easily implemented. Just as important, she wasn't afraid to ask for help. Despite her CIA training and field experience, her best plan was simply to obtain assistance.

Victoria's scenario could play out in any large city or crowded center and provides a great example of a successful hasty plan without a dramatic climax. Unfortunately, sometimes that isn't the case because the conditions and environment are already violent or extreme. Should you find yourself in a situation that is extreme in the truest sense of the word, as I have, even something as simple as dashing 100 yards still requires the basic fundamentals of a plan.

Mogadishu, Somalia

I was sweating under a combat load of twenty pounds including body armor and ammunition, with another sixty pounds of communications equipment on my back in a rucksack. Around me a firefight was taking place that was positively Hollywood in its violence. Rocket-propelled grenades were coming at us from multiple directions and the volume of machine-gun and small arms fire, incoming and out-going, was deafening. It was October 3, 1993, and I was immersed in one of the most violent gunfights in half a century.

As a veteran of the bloody street fighting that day at the Battle of Mogadishu, also widely known as Black Hawk Down, I can attest not only to the bravery of the many American special operations veterans involved but also the necessity of focus when things are at their absolute worst. In the middle of one of the fiercest gunfights since the Vietnam War, I was faced with a dire situation under heavy fire. A friend of mine named Howie, an operator from SEAL Team Six, was lying 200 feet down a dirt alley side street halfway between the good guys and the bad guys. He'd been shot and was severely wounded. He needed help, but I certainly had no desire to put myself in a carnival shooting gallery between the shooters and the targets. It was so exposed I knew I'd likely get shot if I went down there, but I also knew this: If I didn't go down there, Howie would surely die. I needed a plan.

I built one in my mind in a few hasty seconds. First, I needed assistance, someone who could treat Howie (my job involved not only engaging in the combat but controlling airstrikes and command and control communications, and I didn't dare spare much time in the midst of the biggest gunfight of my life). I got the attention of a Delta Force medic named Bob, who was on the far side of the inter-section our team was occupying. Second, I needed to decide what to do with Howie. And that was it, the complete plan. My end state was to retrieve Howie and drag him to medical assistance. I just had to get there and get us back alive. In short, I'd need to act.

Far away from a combat zone and a decade later, Hector in the Shop an' Spend was about to be faced with his own decision about what to do in a crisis. And like me, he found himself responsible for the life of another person, only in his case it was a complete stranger and his plan had the potential to either save or cost the lives of everyone involved.

Canoga Park, California

The Shop an' Spend store has been effectively seized. Hector is watching the two teens who've appeared at the front of the store. Both of whom have pulled semiautomatic pistols as one announced to the stunned shoppers, "Do what we say! Everyone get to the back of the store. Everybody! Do it!"

Hector was immediately possessed by the urge to run (the simplest plan). The exit was thirty feet away and in the opposite direction from the robbers, who were even farther away, but he hesitated to enact this simple plan.

"Everyone get to the back now!"

A stunned Hector found himself falling in behind the two clerks, the manager, and the other three customers as they all trudged like automatons, herded to the back of the store and into the women's restroom. He saw no sign of the other robbers on the way. Once in the restroom, the two teens issued a rush of instructions and threats. "Look at the floor. Look at the walls. Don't look at us!" Immediately the threats escalated and one of the criminals began hitting people. Both became increasingly more drunk on power with each passing minute.

Hector began to fear for himself and the others. He managed a few furtive glances and assessed the other hostages. A teen girl, another thirtysomething male like himself, two other customers, and a couple of twentyish employees, one male the other female. Suddenly the other two criminals burst in. They'd emptied the tills.

"C'mon man, let's go!" But the two hostage takers weren't ready yet. In fact, now they were debating raping the teen girl. The debate escalated into an argument. As they argued, the first pistol-wielding criminal grabbed the teen customer and settled the issue by dragging her into one of the bathroom stalls and kicking the door closed as she screamed and pleaded for help. It was then that Hector made firm eye contact with one of the twentysomething-year-old employees.

The female criminal shouted at the others, and she was clearly angry. "This wasn't the plan! We've got the money! Let's go!"

As they argued, the female victim was shouting, yelling, "He's taking off my clothes! Help me! Please! Oh my God!"

In the confined space of the women's restroom the tension was unbelievable. However, the female and the fourth criminal were through waiting around and wanted no part of the attack. They ran from the bathroom, leaving the rapist in the stall and the last criminal guarding it with his pistol. In the chaos and escalating argument, Hector began a transformation. The married father of none could hear everything in the stall and saw the disbelief in the other victims. He looked toward the same twentysomething-year-old employee again and their eyes locked.

Like many others before him have when under duress, Hector devised a plan in a flash for the simple yet profound reason that if he didn't, something unspeakable and unallowable was going to take place and he didn't have any option but to act—and quickly. Without fully thinking through what might happen after or even during his plan, he decided to disarm the teen with the gun by over-powering him and stopping the other from raping an innocent girl. Plans are rarely more simple or urgent (hasty) than Hector's. All that remains is for him to act. The question is, Does the other person he needs, the twentysomething employee, have the courage as well?

COMMUNICATE YOUR PLANS

Much of the advice I use to paint the safest picture possible revolves around thinking, planning, and actions you take by yourself. But a key component of your safety frequently rests with others. When it comes to personal safety planning, passing information is central.

If you've made plans, they should be communicated to others such as husbands, wives, grown kids, friends or coworkers, the more the better. Deliberate and hasty plans are even more important to share. That's primarily because if you're making them, it's in response to a threat, real or potential. Here I'd like to emphasize the importance of something: If there's a threat that feels real (your SA and Intuition have kicked in), the number one communication you should make is to contact the authorities. This is why preplanning when you're overseas is so important, because you should program or have memorized the number of the local police emergency line. Not find yourself asking the question, as your author did while some assholes stole his Baja 1000 race gear, "Is 9-1-1 the number in Mexico?"

If you've determined you have a problem, you're not bothering the police or being silly by asking them to come to where you are. It's what they do. If calling the authorities feels like overkill (and always use your best judgment), then at least ring someone else on your contact list to update them. An alternative to the police is to use employees or managers.

PLANNING EXERCISES

Use these as examples that can be adapted to your own life and circumstances and by doing so improve your personal planning ability. Bruce Lee Junior and Sleeve Tattoo are out there, not the two that we met in Las Vegas, who've no doubt gone on to prove their manliness through assault and imprisonment yet again, but your local variety of creep.

Scenario 1: My Dinner with Andre Part II

This is a deliberate situation. Like Rule 2 (Trust and Use Your Intuition), pick a restaurant (preferably with windows or, better still, mirrors) and sit down for a nice meal. Now imagine someone is waiting for you between where you're sitting and your destination, whether it be your car, home, or hotel. You've got time because you're safe while you remain in place. This person isn't enough of a threat for you to call the authorities, so imagine you've already informed a friend or family member of your situation. And now it's time to leave. The exercise's objective is this: How do you get to your destination?

Start by drawing on the information and questions you've learned so far. Can you leave by a back entrance and give them the slip? Would the restaurant allow you to do so? Go ahead and ask them, see what they say. Is there anyone you can recruit to help you? Would a restaurant employee or manager be willing? Possibly to even escort you back? What alternate routes are available? What alternative means of transportation are available?

Scenario 2: The Devil Now Wants Your Prada

This scenario takes place while shopping or sightseeing. Go anywhere with crowds or at least enough people that you can choose someone or a group as potential threats. Put yourself in a situation such as inside a store, where you can formulate deliberate plans and consider your options because the interior affords you a certain degree of safety.

You'll find yourself asking the same questions as in Scenario 1.

Can you leave by a back entrance and give them the slip? Would the store allow you to do so? Is there anyone you can recruit to help you? Would a store employee or manager be willing? To even escort you, possibly? And so forth.

Next time, switch it up. While you're walking, pick a moment and imagine someone is following you with criminal intentions. Or have a friend surprise you by selecting an individual. Are you prepared to dial the police? If you're in a foreign country, do you even know (unlike me in Mexico) the number? Where do you need to go to be fully safe, is it home or your hotel? Alternatively, where's the nearest safe place you could duck into? If none, is there someone or a group you see around you that you believe might help?

Scenario 3: Raiders of the Lost Parked

Your car and parking lots are situations worth exploring because, particularly if you're an American, you're likely in and out of your vehicle a lot. Parking lots are common locations for attacks, from rape to robbery, or theft of your vehicle. As you are walking to your car, imagine that someone was following you but you lost them and don't know if they are waiting in the parking lot. As always, begin with the end in mind: What is it you need to do right now?

Always available to you is your default option: Call the police and ask them to come. Trust me, it'd be the easiest call they get that day. Also remember that you don't have to get to your car at that moment necessarily, unless you've somewhere to be. In which case it's a great opportunity for you to make a hasty plan.

Where are the places your creeper would most likely wait to ambush you? Near your car? Near the parking entrance? Are there stairwells you have to pass through that serve as unavoidable choke points? Has the sun set, making the lighting where you parked different than you anticipated? Again, use your imagination to consider questions that apply to your situation.

If you don't have somewhere to be, can you find a nearby safe place? Never feel compelled to rush when you have the option not to. Waiting or coming back later are perfectly reasonable. If you're American, do what a European would do: Go for an espresso. This is a great way to turn a hasty plan into a deliberate one, a fantastic option.

And then, when you do decide to approach your car with the understanding that you don't know where your creeper is, you can be better prepared with your keys in hand, both so you don't have to fumble and also as a convenient weapon.

CONCLUSION

The stories from this chapter provide a variety of examples across a broad spectrum, from extreme combat to a casual get-together (albeit with rock stars). The common theme of course is that in each example the people involved had plans, sometimes hasty or made on the spot, others thought out in advance.

Dutch and I implemented deliberate plans under very different conditions. He knew his destination and the likely types of attack and planned accordingly, returning safely despite credible terrorist and criminal threat. Sitting down to watch the Super Bowl, I had no idea I'd need a plan to counter threats (my SA level was low), but when the potential threat presented itself I still made deliberate plans, even though they were formed on the spot.

Victoria, Hector, and I each made hasty plans under duress. Victoria arguably had the most available time and control over her environment, but that didn't mean she had the luxury of time. In Mogadishu, I was confronted with limited choices and very compressed time in which to consider a plan. This scenario and Victoria's are more similar than they may first appear because we were both experienced risk calculators and highly trained professionals. It is Hector who was most impressive. Faced with a situation that afforded no time for contemplation and without the benefit of experience, he formulated the most simple of plans in the face of grave personal danger.

In the end, know that anything can be a plan, from the most elaborate to the simple or even incomplete. Your plan in a crisis might even seem foolish or unlikely. That is not the way to think of it, because making and having a plan—any plan—is better than *no* plan. It is only with a plan that you can do what's needed in a crisis: Act.

PART III

ACT

RULE FIVE

———

ACT DECISIVELY

WHAT IS A HERO?

COURAGE. AUDACITY. RESOLVE. HEROISM. THESE ARE POWERFUL WORDS, traits that we associate with extraordinary people. Or conversely, people in extraordinary circumstances who have mysteriously tapped into some secret super ability. Either way, never ourselves.

We put heroes and their actions on a pedestal, they reside in some mythological Greek pantheon and we, as mere mortals, reside, well...elsewhere. In the light of public perception and popular fiction, it's a natural conclusion. And one I completely disagree with.

I am going to share with you a secret, one I've come to know absolutely through personal experience. Courage and heroism are simply focusing on what you know you need to do, no matter the risk or personal threat, when it's necessary. That's it. Necessity: the great secret of heroism.

It is a fine thing to read about others and their courage or heroics because they inspire us. However, the important thing for you to understand about the secret to heroism is that anyone is capable of rising to action when in need. That includes you.

Salt Lake City, Utah

Carol DaRonch was about to die. The shy eighteen-year-old had allowed herself to be lured into a car with notorious serial killer Ted Bundy who, realizing that Carol was no longer buying his police officer ruse, had lurched his VW Bug up onto a curb on a darkened street and was trying to slap handcuffs on her.

Suddenly she was possessed by fierce anger that this man thought he could just take her like that, and she fought to get out of the car. A strange realization energized her. "I thought, *My parents are never going to know what happened to me.*" So she took action, fought her way out, managed to get the passenger door open, and fell out onto the curbside grass. Bundy pursued her, pulling out the crowbar he had hidden in the back seat, and pressed his attack. The two struggled on the grass in the chill night air. "He was trying to hit me over the head with it."

But Carol broke free. "I really don't know how I got away. I was so small. And I just think I had this strength that came from somewhere." That somewhere is not nowhere. It is inside all of us. And in the moment when she needed it most, a million years of evolution and survival instinct came to Carol DaRonch's aid. Yet in the end, the rescue was all her doing.

At the climax of their struggle, as Carol managed to break away, Wilbur and Mary Walsh, a local couple in their sixties, were passing by on their way to the grocery store. The petite brunette dashed in front of their car, materializing out of the misty night like an apparition. Startled, Wilbur slammed on the brakes, and Mary, thinking they were under attack, reached for the door lock. But before she could push it, Carol was inside the car with them and Wilbur hit the gas. When they got a look at the girl, they realized something terrible had happened. Recalled Mary, "She was kind of mumbling, 'I can't believe it, I can't believe it.' So that's why I put my arm around her, and I tried to calm her." They asked if she wanted them to try and follow Bundy or take her home. Instead she mustered the courage to say, "Take me to the police station." And with that the couple delivered her to the authorities and her destiny as the "girl who got away."

Adrenaline is a wonderful thing. It allows you to accomplish amazing feats of courage and even strength, but it is not a plan. What it should be is a supplement to one. Even though she had no plan, her instinct (that primal fight-or-flee, urgent, and adrenaline-fueled capability) transformed her need for survival into a supercharged ability to act. Carol saved her own life by taking decisive action.

Mogadishu, Somalia

In the midst of an intense firefight, I was running down a street, directly at my enemy, still weighed down by my eighty pounds of gear. It sounds courageous, but that's not how I view it. I knew I was the one who could do what needed to be done. And I knew the plan, rudimentary as it was: Run like hell to Howie, grab him by his gear harness, drag him back to the (admittedly relative) safety of our own force, turn him over to our medic. So, deep breath, I moved as rapidly as I could while firing rounds into the intersection on the far side of Howie to keep the enemy suppressed, trusting my ability to do the simple things I needed to and luck to keep me safe. I can still clearly recall the surge of energy that hit me as I moved, sweating and weighed down by my load, toward my wounded teammate. I can see the dusty street, the whitewashed adobe walls of the alley, Howie lying on his side in the dirt.

When I arrived I was surprised to find Bob the medic at my

shoulder, yet I shouldn't have been—courage was something I found myself surrounded by for the next eighteen hours of fighting. I shot a couple of enemy fighters, then looked down to find Bob had dropped his medical bag and was prepping Howie's leg. However, our point-blank shooting gallery was not the place to start treatment. In other words, it wasn't a good idea to change my initial plan. "*Fuck* that. Drag him around the corner," I said. Without waiting for a response, I grabbed Howie by his H-gear (what we called the harnesses we wore for combat at the time) and began dragging him on his back toward friendly lines. He was heavily weighted down with gear and I strained, but I never changed my focus from that second, and now current, step of my plan: to drag him to safety. In my mind's eye I can see my feet and Howie in the dirt, his shattered leg leaving blood on the street. It was taking forever. Until suddenly I was back at our intersection and I was able to get him out of the crossfire. I unceremoniously propped Howie against the nearest wall and left him in the care of Bob, then went back to doing my job.

You can accomplish extraordinary feats of courage too. And you *will*, when the time comes. You'll be best served, as I was, by having a plan. Don't leave it till too late, as Carol did. The question you're probably asking yourself is how? How in a crisis do I summon that needed courage?

FOCUS ON YOUR PLAN

Once you have a plan, even a hasty one formed in a matter of seconds, there's nothing more to think about. It's time to take action. That's it. Do it. Act. Just as I did in the streets of Mogadishu. Just as Carol, a demure teen without combat experience, did on a Salt Lake City street.

There's a special ops maxim: Speed, audacity, and violence of action win the day. I've lived and survived by this maxim in extreme combat. Trust me when I say that while your potential perpetrator may have experience with their particular crime, they're going to be scared. More likely, they aren't experienced and are in fact anxious, and possibly under the effects of either alcohol or drugs (Bundy drank heavily before his attacks), which can be to your advantage. Seize the initiative and turn the tables on your assailant by being quick and decisive in your actions. Take *them* by surprise. Your decisiveness and the element of surprise make it instantly clear you're willing to engage them, without actually making physical contact. It also serves as a deterrent to physical struggle. Believe me when I say you'll shock them, and in that instant, as their confidence evaporates, you'll be in command. Congratulations. And remember, there is no fair fight when it comes to crime and threats. You must use and exploit *every* advantage.

This may seem easy to say but difficult to do when faced with a dire situation. The best way to overcome that fear is to revert to your plan. It's the reason to make plans in advance before anything happens. By having one, you *know* what to do. You're prepared and can act decisively. Start by pausing here and thinking about the first step of one of the plans you made in the exercise scenarios for Rule 4. Focus on one specific plan you made. If you're willing to take an extra minute, write down the steps that get you from your threat situation to your safe destination.

What was the first step that required you to move or take an action? Picture yourself in that situation and doing what you need to do first. Congratulations again, you've just identified your source of personal courage. In real life, your plan can, and often will, become your or someone else's lifesaver. It's also okay for the plan to change along the way, so that your actions are different than you may have originally thought. By focusing on what to do next, you can suppress panic and fear because you're already focusing on what you *can* do, not what *might* happen to you or that which is outside your control. These are the sources of your fear and can short-circuit your ability to take action.

Canoga Park, California

Shop an' Spend store hostage Hector was trapped in the women's restroom with a handful of other victims. A pistol-wielding teen held them at gunpoint while his accomplice was attempting to rape one of the female hostages in a stall. The two other perpetrators had taken the money and fled.

In the stall, the terrified girl was still pleading for help as her attacker tore her clothing off and tried to rape her. Her pleading then turned to sobbing. Hector and the employee who'd made eye contact nodded to each other. They simply couldn't let a girl be raped while standing fifteen feet away. And in their nod, he and the employee exchanged all the information needed. Hector can't say who moved first, but it doesn't matter. They charged the armed sentry. The shocked criminal fought, but the two determined men, who in the course of acting *knew* what they needed to do, battered him and the gun went flying. It slid across the floor as the two men, ordinary people acting from necessity, became heroes. Another hostage, unfamiliar with firearms, nonetheless picked up the pistol to keep it away from the criminal as Hector and his partner subdued the sentry.

Outside the restroom in the store, the shelf stocker who'd been hiding during the commotion saw the two fleeing criminals and came out. He entered the bathroom in the midst of the all-out brawl. His coworker and Hector were now struggling with the would-be rapist, who was completely surprised and likely so focused on trying to rape the girl that he failed to realize the tables had turned before it was too late. The other hostages, now galvanized, were fighting with the sentry. Someone took the opportunity to call the police. In the pandemonium the would-be rapist broke loose and fled the store. The last criminal, now completely outnumbered, was subdued and locked in the women's bathroom to await the police.

If Hector and the others had not acted, it's difficult to say what might have happened. Certainly the girl would have been raped. My experience with men who turn violent is that once they cross a certain line, they are capable of even greater atrocity. It's possible that after raping her they might have decided to kill everyone. A convenient and easily accomplished crime with everyone trapped in a single room and two perpetrators with pistols. Countless studies have confirmed that criminals in power (particularly younger males) only become more violent, especially if there are more than one.

The truth is, if there's a threat you should expect it to come from a male or group of males. I've certainly encountered demonic females in my own travels and at frighteningly close proximity. But for violence and criminal activity (and the worst combination, violent criminals), you have to look to men. A group of violent female criminals is so rare you're as likely to be elected prime minister of a small European country as find one. For as far back as can be reliably determined, the violence associated with our social history as a species has been driven by males and is most pronounced when they're in packs or large numbers.

To quote Wrangham and Peterson in regard to violence in groups of primates (including us), "Here is the fear you feel on an empty street when the muggers step out from the shadows, the same quick arithmetic that may enter the minds of criminal and victim simultaneously, the same acknowledgment of the importance of numbers."

That is why using numbers if you have them—or finding them if you don't—is such an important action. In the meantime, let's look at a couple victims who did not have the benefit of numbers and see how they fare when faced with a crisis. Not far from our would-be Shop an' Spend rapist is another.

Venice Beach, California

Joe Keesling was still loose and working the nearby beach communities in search of victims. He'd already unsuccessfully attacked Ashley in her community laundry room after she unwisely let him into the apartment complex but thwarted him when she successfully fought him with all her ability (action) and screamed to bring others to her aid, refusing to be a victim. After he fled (as the coward he is) he made contact with his second target, Patty, at her apartment complex gate, but as we learned, she's not as foolish about entry as Ashley, and when he pressed her to let him in that's when she took her first action, albeit verbal.

Later that night, when he attempted his break-in through her bedroom, she took her second and more courageous action. That is, she refused to give up and fought him off. In so doing, and in my expert opinion, Patty became a hero. Detective Starsky agrees. She knows that to fight and then report an attack are both, independently, courageous acts. The LAPD was now alerted to Joe's presence even if they didn't know who he was, yet. And because Patty got a good look at his face from mere inches away as they fought through her bedroom window, Starsky had a solid description.

Twice thwarted, Joe went in search of his next victim (like

rapists and criminals everywhere, he continued unless permanently stopped). He'd been frustrated twice and was angry. Two women had prevented him from getting what he felt he was owed: compliant victims. Two weeks later he again made what had become his standard approach.

Madison was another young woman in her twenties with semi-blonde hair, coming home from work, and as she opened her apartment complex gate Joe asked her to let him in. This time he'd waited for a victim who came home later, after seven p.m., when it was already dark outside.

"Sure," she said, noting his creepy vibe but, unlike Patty, shrugging it off and letting him in. She went straight to her apartment but felt as though "the guy at the gate was watching me." Unlike the other two victims, Madison had a roommate, but she'd gone out for the evening on a date. Madison, who had to work first thing in the morning, decided to go to sleep early. Their apartment, like the previous victims', was on the ground floor with windows that faced outside of the complex. Around ten p.m. she was awakened by a noise. Thinking it was in the kitchen and therefore her roommate, Madison went back to sleep.

She nodded off, only to be startled awake by a man already on top of her in her bed. She was instantly fighting, but it was too late. Though she was smaller than the two other women, she never gave up and managed to bite and scratch him in their fight. He finished and left quickly out the front door.

Madison was both a fortunate and unfortunate victim. She was fortunate in that, by sheer luck of the draw, her rapist wasn't also a murderer like Ted Bundy. Unfortunate because, unlike the other two victims, she didn't give herself the opportunity to act in time to prevent the attack. However, it's never too late to act, even when you're already under attack. Fighting like Madison did, or any type of action really, is beneficial and can be critical. Because if you don't act and therefore allow yourself to be controlled by a perpetrator or perpetrators, you are giving over control of your very life to someone else. Madison not only never gave up, but even though she didn't prevent her rape, she had the courage to notify the police. And we'll see how in the course of her actions (by biting and scratching) she exacted some justice.

How to Channel Your Inner Badass

The purpose of Rule 5 is for you to be best equipped should you find yourself in a situation that necessitates action. When I first decided to write this book, I knew that the best approach was to draw not solely from my own expertise but also from that of the three distinct communities I've had the pleasure of serving in, alongside, or encountering along my journey. Their collective wisdom permeates *The Power of Awareness*, but perhaps nowhere does that expertise have more value for individual personal safety than in how to take action.

Understanding speed, audacity, and violence of action, and other maxims drawn from the world of US special operations forces (SOF):

1. The first tip, and one I'd emphasize above others, is the SOF adage of "speed, audacity, and violence of action." It's been around in some form or other for ages, with entire martial tomes dedicated to it. It's even written into the US Army's *Operations* field manual (FM 100-5). Check it out if you ever need help sleeping, because field manuals are anything but compelling

reading. That aside, the adage doesn't imply that you need to be violent necessarily, rather that you are fully committed to your action. By combining your plan with your commitment, you can act more decisively and that gives you the initiative. And initiative means you're in control.

2. Related but separate from the above is to go with your compulsion. When you feel a compulsion to act in a certain way or to take a certain course of action, listen to it. That compelling urge most likely springs from your Intuition and instinct (fight or flee). If those two are speaking to you, it's for the reason that Intuition always asserts itself: It's trying to save your life. Listen.

3. Face your enemies. Attacks of a personal nature almost always come from behind or at least from where or when you're not looking. Ted Bundy did this most of the time. If you can't get away from them (and simply getting away is almost always the best action if possible), facing them affords you certain advantages.

4. Search for teammates. What I mean here is you should always be looking for others who can help you. We've established that numbers matter in a crisis, but the types of numbers can be just as important. One lone cop can make all the difference even when compared to a group of civilians, but know that anyone in an official capacity such as parking lot attendants or managers can change the

tide of events decisively as well. Nevertheless, the more people the better.

Applying your inner James Bond, by Victoria, former CIA case officer:

1. We've already established that staring in rapt oblivion at your phone is not to your advantage when you're in situations that could be dangerous. However, knowing that you *will* still do so, here's how you can rapidly turn it to your advantage. If you're being followed or think you're going to be confronted, use it. Cops first, always, if you can. But no matter, dial someone. Better yet, put them on speakerphone because doing so lets them hear what is going on, which may be of benefit later (see Rule 6) but also makes it seem to the perpetrator that more people are involved, because they are. It's a subtle but effective psychological trick of human nature. And if you can't get anyone on the phone? Pretend. "Baby! You'll be here in three minutes? Great, because there's this asshole here who's bothering me..." You'll know what to do to earn that Oscar award for best actress or actor in a dramatic role.

2. Engage your enemy. Victoria and other female case officers I've known understand that you can turn the tables psychologically by initiating the dialogue rather than waiting for them. Ask them aggressively, "Can I help you?" "Why are you following me?" and don't be afraid to throw in an expletive, because that too will change how people see you, and giving

them any kind of pause is good. "Is there a fucking problem?"[6]

3. When not to act. With many years and operations overseas, Victoria recommends an important, somewhat counterintuitive tip. In her time in Kenya, a country rife with robbers and carjackers, she learned that when someone wants your possessions but not you, give them over.[7] "There were roundabouts in Nairobi (Kenya's capital) where you could expect to get carjacked in certain traffic conditions. I knew a guy who, after he got jacked, actually asked the robber if he could keep his cell phone so he could call someone to pick him up, and his carjacker let him keep it." We'll talk more about strategies to counter or thwart robberies and other crimes in Tool 1, Preparedness.

How not to be a crime victim, by Detective Starsky, LAPD:

1. If you find yourself in doubt, stop. Things such as, "I'm not sure I should _____." (Fill in that blank with anything you can imagine: "let him in"; "open my door"; "let him buy me a drink.") When doubts like these arise, it probably means you need to take action. Regardless, stop and assess if you have a problem.

---

6   I like the word "fuck" because the letter "f" purses the lips and it's short as well as unambiguous. Plus it shows them you're not fucking around.

7   Giving them your possessions, including your car, is not the same as giving them control of you or your body, something you should never do.

2. Act early, don't delay. Hector could have saved himself and others from potential harm had he dropped
   everything and immediately left the checkout counter.
   Outside he could have dialed the police and changed
   the robbers' and the rapist's dynamic completely. Carol
   DaRonch, despite falling for Ted Bundy's ruse initially,
   could have had her altercation and made her escape
   while still in the mall parking lot. She later recounted,
   "I knew I made a mistake as soon as I got in the car,"
   but failed to act.

3. By acting, you take power from your perpetrator.
   Anything you do that disrupts their plan is in your
   interest. At a minimum, it throws off their plan. At
   best, it can stop them outright. As Detective Starsky
   says, "Throw them off their plan or their game. It
   causes them to lose their ability to follow through."
   This is something she's seen over and over in twenty-
   five years of fighting crime.

4. Never stop fighting. If you're attacked, fighting, as
   Carol DaRonch, Ashley, Patty, and Madison all did,
   makes a difference. Sometimes it works, and sometimes
   it may not. But you will know you did all you could.
   This is an important consideration and we'll discuss it
   in great depth in the next chapter.[8] "You never stop
   fighting because you don't know when they might

---

8   I've experienced this firsthand in combat, when things have not turned out as
     I'd hoped, and someone died, or we failed. Regardless of the outcome, I still
     know that I never gave up until it was finished. It may seem like little solace,
     but it's important.

quit (as in Patty's case) and they don't know when you will. You want them to feel that you won't give up." Criminals have consistently told her that "fighters" always cause them trouble and may draw attention to the situation and can in fact be frightening to them. In the end, it's a personal decision you'll have to make, but criminal experts and I agree there is very little downside in fighting and zero upside in submission (the exception being property theft).

CONCLUSION

When you find yourself in circumstances that are intimidating or threatening, if you have a plan, then your actions are already clear. And remember, the plan you have is the best plan available. Don't doubt it; believe it. Use it to save your life. And don't stop until you've reached safety or obtained the assistance you need. Start with the thing you need to do first. Then the next and so forth. In doing so, if the circumstances require, you will be a hero. Either your own or someone else's. That's how it works.

Rule 5 and the actions you take are the culmination of everything you've learned in this book so far, and the rule is designed to keep you safe when you're most at risk—*during* the crisis. Even if you haven't memorized the other rules, much of what you need to do in a time of action is resident in you already. My hope, if nothing else, is that in coming to understand that inherent power a bit better you'll be more confident and capable of taking action.

There are no exercises for this chapter. That's because the practical knowledge and practice you need are already contained in the previous rules. I encourage you to return to those chapters and practice the exercises associated with each. But don't stop there.

Build on them. Ultimately, only your familiarity in drawing on your Situational Awareness, Intuition, and skill in planning will give you the best chance of taking appropriate action and emerging safely. The more you practice and apply and tailor your newfound skills to your own life, the greater that likelihood. So, take the time and use your imagination.

Once you've acted, there remains one final step when dealing with a threat or crisis, and it's important to understand that even when you're out of immediate danger you're still not finished. It's critical to personal recovery, peace of mind, and your sense of justice to follow up, something we'll explore the reasons for, and means to accomplish, in greater detail in the final rule: The Two Rs.

RULE SIX

THE TWO RS— REGROUP & RECOVER

Somewhere on the Arabian Peninsula

BAM! BAM! BAM! THREE GUNSHOTS HAVE JUST SHATTERED THE PLEASANT bustle of the Arab marketplace, leaving a tight spiderweb of broken glass in the passenger window of Billy's car. The assassin has disappeared into the crowd without so much as a backward glance.

In Billy's SUV the brief and deafening silence was immediately replaced by the bustle of expertise in action. They needed to move. Now. If anything else was going to happen it would be here, right where they were sitting. Perhaps in the next few seconds. To remain in place was to invite death.

The driver put the car in gear (the engine was already running) and quickly pulled out into traffic while the others continued eyeing their surroundings for the next threat. Billy rapidly scanned through the windows, including the fractured passenger glass, for what would come next, most likely an explosive-laden vehicle to kill all of them. One of the team reported the assassination attempt via cell phone and relayed the most critical information: where the team was, no one was injured, and they were returning to their clandestine safe house. Weaving through vehicle congestion and leaving the stunned crowd behind, Billy and his team disappeared into the dust and commerce of the Arabian heat.

REGROUPING

Billy and his team have just experienced a violent and devastating attempt on their lives. Regardless of how it happened and what they missed in the lead-up, what is most important to ensure their safety is putting distance between themselves and the attack site, then they can take the additional steps necessary to determine if they are still in danger. They ignore everything else, including their earlier mistakes, and focus only on what they need to do.

In effect, the team is regrouping.

First, Run

In any potential threat, confrontation, or attack, the most important action you can take is to remove yourself. As I stated in the introduction, I eschew blanket computations and calculations; however, there is one formula I embrace and it's the only math you'll need to understand in this entire book. It's expressed in this equation: distance = safety. Learn it, know it, live it. The fact is, the farther you are from danger and the sooner you distance yourself from the threat, the safer you are. Our now Shop an' Spend hero Hector would have been safest if he'd simply walked away (avoiding a potential attack does not make one a coward) from the checkout counter when his Intuition told him he should; because outside the store equaled a safe standoff distance. He could then have called in reinforcements by way of the police and still been the hero. Distance is so important that I initially titled Rule 6 "The Three Rs" to incorporate Run as a separate and first post-incident action.

You can also think of running as a reminder that being out of the immediate kill zone (as we refer to ambush sites in the military) is not the same as safety. Keep moving—on foot, by train, in your car—because distance (i.e., running away) is the best safety protocol for ensuring you're not still subject to attack or pursuit. It also applies to situations where someone has tried to enter your home or duped you into opening the gate to your apartment complex. Escaping your property could prove to be the safest course of action. Or it could be that safety lies in making a getaway in your car just as Billy's team did, because, let's be honest, even professional counterterrorists run away when it's called for.

Regroup

After you've escaped or avoided a bad situation is not the time to make the novice mistake of letting your guard down or trying to get back to normal right away. If the occurrence felt truly threatening, you're going to be experiencing an adrenaline rush or the hangover effect from one—a feeling of fatigue and a desire to disengage. This is precisely the time to maintain your vigilance.

Regrouping means taking stock of your situation and collecting your wits. Once you're out of that kill zone, begin asking questions. What are your new surroundings? Are you fully safe from your threat? Have you arrived at your desired or final destination? Is now the time to call the police, or someone else? If you're with others, check those with you to make sure they're okay, emotionally as well as physically.

Regrouping is nothing more than applying the rules you've already learned as part of staying safe. Look around, be Situationally Aware of your new environment. Listen to your Intuition, heightened as it is from what just happened, and assess your new situation. And if you're not completely out of the woods, simply refer back to your rules. Perhaps you find yourself at Rule 3, determining whether you *still* have a problem (could the perpetrators still be after you?) or perhaps a new one (you're in a different and possibly unsafe part of town). If so, then proceed to Rule 4 and make another plan. Then take action (Rule 5).

Regrouping and running need not necessarily be separate or mutually exclusive. You might regroup shortly after escape and then realize what needs to happen next is to put even more distance between yourself and the incident. And while running can be literally just that, running for your life, distance remains the key. Criminals pick a spot to attack and, as a general rule, will only pursue a victim so far before giving up, for the same reason there is value in fighting as part of Rule 5: The more they pursue you or continue to try, the more exposed they are, and criminals do not like exposure. The key here is moving until you *feel* safe—relying on your Intuition and instincts. Listen to them. Then you can take stock and begin to process what has happened.

RECOVERY

Reporting

In the course of recovering from an incident, the first—though oft undesirable—step is to engage the authorities. You need to report what happened. This can often be difficult for civilians. In special ops we're fanatical about following up with After-Action Reports and conducting hotwashes. ("Hotwash" is a term in my community that came from standing planeside while you dissected a just-completed operation—essentially rehashing events and actions while they are so fresh in everyone's mind that the props are still turning and the engine exhaust "washes" over you. It has come to represent the earnest delving into mistakes and successes by everyone involved.) It's how we improve, but also how we avoid repeating mistakes in the life-and-death consequence of special operations.

If you experienced theft or were actually attacked and got away, it's important to ensure the authorities know for three reasons. First, it's the only way to bring the perpetrator(s) to justice and prevent them from potentially harming others. Second, it's a formal means of hotwashing, allowing you to go over the events and learn from them. Life goes on and there is value in understanding how you can avoid mistakes and improve. Third, it is part of full recovery and a healthy healing process. I've experienced some extremely violent combat in my career. And those experiences will be with me for life, just as they are for other combat veterans and civilian victims of crime. I've spent extensive time analyzing and sharing post-combat or operations assessments and outcomes. I was Billy's commander at the time of his near assassination, and we spent a great deal of time analyzing the operation, the conditions leading up to it, and the outcomes. These things, while sometimes painful, help.

Reporting also tells your subconscious that you're taking action, and this act can help diminish trauma. Even if nothing comes from your actions within the justice system or through other authorities, you've done something about the attack, you've taken the action. I can't overstate this enough, so I'll repeat it. Whether you feel justice was served or a future attack on someone else prevented or not, your mind knows you did the right and just thing, and that is psychologically beneficial. The necessity of doing so does not in any way diminish the difficulty or even retraumatization that can accompany notifying police or other authorities such as university officials or medical professionals. Whether the crime will be prosecuted, justice served, your account taken seriously, or you are blamed for your own traumatic experience are all legitimately intimidating and frightening prospects. And nothing I say here changes that. But Detective

Starsky, with years of working sex crimes in addition to robbery and burglary, shared with me advice on the importance of reporting: "You owe it to yourself to give us the chance to bring suspects to justice. Otherwise, if no one knows, they will one hundred percent have gotten away with it."

Venice Beach, California

Ashley, Patty, and Madison had three separate experiences with rapist Joe Keesling. What they had in common was the nerve to report the incident. Had Ashley not, Detective Starsky would never have known he was targeting the area. Had Patty not, then Starsky wouldn't have had an eyewitness who could positively identify his face, because Madison never saw it. Madison, bravest of all, provided the final and irrefutable DNA that, when combined with the sample from under Ashley's fingernails and the marks she left on him by fighting, led to his arrest and delivered the guilty verdict (all three women testified against him in court) that put him in state prison where, hopefully, he got to experience firsthand the receiving end of his own crime for the next decade.

Canoga Park, California

When the police arrived at the Shop an' Spend and took the sentry criminal into custody, the testimony and assistance of Hector (and all the victims) allowed them to connect the other three criminals through gang memberships and allegiances. Ultimately the three males were convicted. The female, who became a witness for the prosecution, was later killed by her gang. Hector learned to never ignore his Intuition and the near rape victim remains grateful to

Hector and the employee whose necessary courage (heroism) while at gunpoint saved her from a greater traumatic experience and possibly death, along with all the other hostages.

There are places where you can't expect results, and you should be prepared for this reality if you travel internationally. As I watched my Baja 1000 race aspirations disappear up a Mexican highway, my expectations for justice weren't high. A crime that in the States would have been stopped in a handful of minutes via rapid radio communications with the Highway Patrol before the thieves could evaporate took an hour for a response, which materialized in the form of two casually disinterested Federales. The first one to speak greeted us with a lazy "¿Qué pasó?" *Oh, I dunno, our vehicles and all our shit currently pulling into a Tijuana chop shop maybe? What's happening with you guys?*

Recovery

Reporting an incident is merely a step toward a more important goal. Recovering in the aftermath of an attack or traumatic close call is the final destination in post-incident well-being. Sometimes events come and go in a flash and leave minimal scar tissue—Ashley's ordeal in her apartment complex laundry room is one of those; while it was traumatic, she didn't linger on her close call. For Madison the memory of her rape has never disappeared; it permanently changed her, but she did recover and went on to get married and start a family. She lives a happy, yet more cautious life.

I've witnessed horrific things and engaged in soul-altering violence in my own life. The scars are permanent. Philosophically speaking, killing people even when it's justified or necessary is always a net negative experience. There's no positive or upside, that I've found at least, and I've spent considerable time in reflection on the subject. I still suffer from survivor's guilt and relive mistakes I've made. And for a very long time I relived certain of the most violent scenes daily until they became weekly, then monthly, and eventually rarely entered my thoughts. The thing about time is it passes. And with it the sharp edges of trauma become rounder, smoother. Both are good things.

My path to recovery from violence has also proved to be a journey without destination. That's not to say I haven't come to some measure of peace, but rather that recovery will forever be an ongoing affair. Every time I arrived at what I thought was the end point, it turned out to be merely a sojourn. Even now, in some cases decades after violence, there are days when I feel rage and even moments when I want to burn the world down without reason. Other times, certain sights or particular songs or smells (which can ambush you without warning) can evoke emotions I'm embarrassed of in public. The national anthem at certain events, cliché as it may sound, is one that gets me under the right conditions, and it has nothing to do with convenient patriotism and everything to do with particular friends I've lost, either to combat or PTSD suicide.

In my life I've found two distinctly separate groups of people and a single philosophical safe harbor to help. The first were teammates I've experienced trauma with, because no one understands better than those who carry the same scars as you. The second is my wife, who knows me better than anyone, including all my flaws and damage, and loves me anyway. While her understanding of combat is nil, her compassion is boundless. And her acceptance absolute. You needn't be married or have combat mates to find this kind of support, however. Support groups comprised of survivors, and professional institutions such as the Department of Veterans Affairs or the National Sexual Assault Telephone Hotline, are places to start. There you can find people who've gone through similar experiences. People who will understand you.

When I was in my darkest place personally, and before I met my wife, the second anchor for my own peace and recovery came in the form of Buddhist temples in Thailand. For a handful of years, I was fortunate to work in and pass through that lovely country regularly and found that sitting in a temple for an hour or two and exploring Theravada Buddhist philosophy brought great relief and peace. It still does. That's because for me it isn't a religion (I am not religious) but a way of understanding the world around me and my experiences. For others, that same solace can be found in religion itself, other philosophies, or practices such as meditation.

What rape survivors, combat veterans, mass shooting victims, and those who have survived other traumas such as car crashes all share is not their experiences, which vary widely, but the necessity and value of pursuing recovery. And you must allow for the passage of time, because it does heal and even sometimes eliminates scars. This book does not provide the expertise for extensive answers or a comprehensive emotional and psychological path to full post-trauma recovery except for the resources in Appendix A and to say this: Seek assistance. I did. And the combat veterans and assault (sexual or other) survivors I know who've recovered best have all leaned on others. If not professionals, then friends and family. It is not beneficial to hold traumatic experiences inside.

Amber Stell is a certified social worker and victim advocate for the Ogden Metro Police Department in Utah with years of experience helping people work through trauma. She says, "It's a false sense of security to hold it inside. Holding it in allows you to revisit it over and over again in an unhealthy way and all alone. I find it opens people up to being victims again."

Instead, Amber believes reaching out and the willingness to share experiences, even painful ones, becomes a self-sustaining cycle of recovery because "When you do [reach out], you gain resiliency and the ability to work through other things as well." In so doing, the burden becomes lighter.

Another step on the journey to recovery can be to face your demons or the personification of them in the form of the perpetrator. Crimes and life don't always afford us that opportunity, for many reasons, but there can be great value in doing so, not only for yourself but for others whom you don't or may never even know.

Aspen, Colorado; Tallahassee, Florida; and Salt Lake City, Utah

Carol DaRonch sat in the chair of the witness stand and faced her would-be killer, Ted Bundy. It was the trial for the murder of twenty-three-year-old nurse Caryn Campbell, who was skiing at the Snowmass Village ski resort when he'd kidnapped her by feigning an injury and luring her into helping him load his ski boots into his car. Her body was found five weeks later. Ted, who'd been extradited to Aspen from Utah after his conviction for Carol's attempted kidnap, wasn't just in the courtroom; he was acting as his own attorney and as such got to cross-examine the now twenty-one-year-old.

"He was so arrogant. I just think he thought he was going to get away with everything." But her commitment to pursuing justice for the other victims gave her the strength to face him, even when he'd try to cast doubt on her testimony, asking her how she could even be sure it was him who'd approached and then attacked her. Looking him squarely in the eye, she left no question that it was.

He was headed for a probable conviction when he escaped during the trial, not once but twice, forever suspending the Colorado case. Once on the run, he headed as far away as he could get by bus, train, plane, and finally stolen car, eventually landing in Florida. After he killed two Florida State sorority members and a twelve-year-old girl, he was apprehended for the final time during a traffic stop in his stolen car. When he went on trial in Tallahassee for the last three murders he'd ever commit, Carol found herself facing him again (he served as his own lawyer for most of his trials). His attempts at intimidation always fell short.

How did she get through facing the man who wanted to kill her and now stared hatred across crowded courtrooms? "I surprised myself of the strength I had to get through all that, but I had a lot of support." In addition to her determination to pursue justice, her last statement confirms the key to long-term recovery, something Amber the professional victim advocate agrees with—get support.

As Carol's story reveals, going to trial can be intimidating and frightening. However, according to Amber, "People who do go through that process to the end, they feel a sense of accomplishment. Of course, no one asks for something terrible to have happened. But when they do get through [court proceedings]—and it is slow, one foot after the other—each step builds confidence and each step is another piece of themselves from before the trauma they get back." Pursuing justice can be a big part of recovery, from justice being served, of course, but also from the standpoint that it allows you to have done something about what happened. It's a big key to long-term recovery and putting things behind you or finding peace.

Aside from infrequent court appearances, Bundy did not occupy mental space in Carol's life. "My relationship with him was purely to make him pay for what he had done." She was therefore "able to detach myself from an event that could have ruined my life." Rather than focus on Ted or the undesired public attention she's received ever since, she focused on living her life. She went to college and earned a degree in business management and enjoyed a career in telecommunications, staying in Utah and raising a small family with the Wasatch Mountains as a backdrop. These days she enjoys golf and her life partner of fifteen years. "I'm really happy and healthy and just live a normal life."

CONCLUSION

The final rule may not be the most critical. But in many ways, it has the most lasting effect. Events don't always work out the way we would like, and for many reasons. Nothing compensates anger, loss, injury, or pain. When my race car was stolen in Mexico, how well did our Federales perform once they were on the scene? Let's just say it was a long and lonely walk across the border twelve hours later in the wee hours of the morning, so thank God for the reasonable US customs agents who let us into the country without passports or, in JT's case, any identification whatsoever. Did we ever hear anything from the Mexican officials about our race truck? Need I answer the question?

Other times it works out wonderfully. Carol DaRonch was fortunate not only to have survived Ted Bundy's attack but to have been determined to remain a thorn in his side, a source of rage for the asshole who'd attacked her. She never wavered in her pursuit of justice on behalf of herself and all his victims. "He didn't deserve to live," she says simply, three decades after his execution. Carol's recovery and happiness were her ultimate revenge, because she's a living, laughing human.

When he finally fried in Florida's state prison on January 24, 1989, he knew he'd never escaped that one young woman as she turned the tables on him in court again and again. It was Carol's courage that brought him to justice for the first time. That single action spelled the beginning of the end for one of the evilest serial killers in history. His last words as they slipped the black hood over his head were: "I really am an asshole." I may be wrong about those last words, but it hardly matters because he really was.

By taking active steps after an incident to ensure you're safely out of harm's way, then regrouping to determine what else, if anything, you need to do next, you have gained control of the situation. When it's all over, muster the courage to report an incident or attack and know that in so doing you've done everything you can. Then you're prepared to move forward with the conviction that you've given justice the best chance to take its course and hopefully helped yourself to gain closure. Always remember, there is no shortcut to time, and combining its passage with the love and support of others (including experts) places you on the path to recovery. It's a long path. Sometimes it can feel pretty bleak, and I've been there. Other times everything can feel sunny and fine. Sometimes it swaps back and forth. Yet, however sunny or dark that path is, I've found, at least, we have to continue walking it. It's just easier if you have someone to walk with.

THE TOOLS

TOOL ONE

PREPAREDNESS

BEING PREPARED IS ALL ABOUT DOING THINGS IN ADVANCE, NEVER in the act. The problem usually is that it's an easy thing to put off, like filing taxes, because, well, there isn't any threat at the moment, so why worry? But putting off preparing the place you live for defense against an invader, getting competent self-defense training to boost your confidence and competence, or purchasing a self-defense tool are all mistakes for the obvious reason that you will never know when that moment each or all are important will arrive.

Consider my Las Vegas Super Bowl game with the Alan Parsons Project. The plan I made in the midst of a potentially lethal confrontation was only sound because of preparations I'd made beforehand, sometimes years in advance: martial arts and other combatives training during my special operations career; knowing how to assess the space I was in, in this case a giant banquet hall and the casino resort that encompassed it; and finally, I was armed with a weapon, a tactical pen.

HOME PREPARATION

Home planning is not complex, but when overlooked can carry potentially disastrous consequences. Reflect on Patty, our second near rape victim from Venice Beach, who for a terrifying moment had to fight off her attacker through the window. She'd never considered her window to be a threat, but understanding that her home bordered the outside perimeter of her apartment complex on the ground floor and planning for that kind of vulnerability could have saved her from the confrontation.

It is important to prepare yourself and your loved ones inside the space you consider safest and most comfortable, where your guard will always be at its lowest: your home. You spend as much time there as anywhere else, and likely feel more at ease there than you would anywhere else. Yet you likely don't have an accurate assessment of its vulnerabilities or attributes and may not have a plan for how to escape or defend it in the event of an invasion or disaster. That's natural. This is your home, and you think of it as the safe space where you are surrounded by familiar things and those you love, not as a place that makes you vulnerable. But if you don't take the time to look at it through the eyes of a predator, you're leaving yourself, your family, and your possessions defenseless.

From a threat standpoint the most likely entry is through doors and windows, and therefore each of these requires your scrutiny. Second- or third-story windows and balconies are also vulnerable, don't assume height is a measure of safety. If you have a garage with an automatic door opener, understand that those handy, convenient gadgets can be spoofed (techno geekery for capturing the electronic signal), depending on the manufacturer and age, though most now use rolling codes to defeat this. Many garage doors can also be forced open with pry bars, and padlocks can be cut with bolt cutters.

Use the Appendix B Home Security checklist to assess your home's vulnerabilities.

Preventing entry is the first step in considering your home's fortification. But if someone is in your home and you don't want to confront them, what will you do? Escape, as always, is the answer, but only if you've thought about it beforehand. Using the Home Security checklist, think about your home's interior layout. If someone broke in while you were asleep, is there a door you can escape through to get outside? A window? What would be the best escape route? Do you have some type of self-defense weapon at hand (because you should always maintain one within arm's reach, not tucked away in the closet or across the room)?

If you hear a noise (that one that wakes you up and, thanks to your new connection to Intuition, tells you something's up), grab that weapon immediately. If you think someone is already in the house, dial 9-1-1 first, tell them you think you have an intruder. If it's a false alarm, don't worry about it, that's what police are paid for. If you do get up to investigate, turn on the lights, there's no sense in sneaking. Announce, "I'm armed, and I will shoot you if you don't leave," even if you don't have a gun. Take along whatever you're armed with and check everywhere. I suggest the standard American baseball bat; they're easy to obtain and holding one makes you intimidating even if you're not. Also take your phone, and if you're on with the police put it on speaker. Remember that scenario in Rule 1 about going through your house with the preconceived notion of "Yup, nothing's here?" Well, now's not the time to skimp on checking every corner.

Rehearsing is key to success in a crisis. Be sure you walk through the scenario above multiple times, adding to it and tailoring it with your own personal details and home particulars. Be inventive and thorough. Where would you go if you fled the house? If you don't know now, you won't know then. At a minimum it should be somewhere with a phone in case, for any reason, you don't have yours.

PUBLIC SPACE AND TRANSPORTATION TIPS

Many Americans don't use public transportation and may find it unfamiliar and intimidating. It can also be confusing and crowded. In those environments it's easy to be less Situationally Aware or to get distracted while you're figuring things out. So, whether you're a seasoned metro or rail rider or in a strange city walking across a crowded plaza, use these tips to ensure you're less likely to be targeted or a victim.

- Don't carry your phone in your back pocket. Don't carry your wallet in your back pocket. Back pockets are known as "sucker" pockets in the criminal world.

- Wear purse straps, satchel straps, etc., cross-body. This helps you to hold the bag closer to, and toward the front of, your body. At a minimum, ensure you have strong straps (cut-resistant or difficult-to-cut material such as heavy-duty Cordura is better than leather or standard nylon, which cut easily when stretched, such as during an attempted snatch), and always keep one hand firmly gripping where the front strap meets the bag.

- For backpacks specifically, do not do the "cool kid" single-shoulder hang. Put both straps on and fasten all chest and waist straps. If you have both, it's nearly impossible for a pack to be pulled off you.

- For females, Victoria recommends tucking a lone ID, credit card, and twenty dollars (or foreign equivalent) inside a bra strap.

- Alternatively, consider putting the same inside your sock. There are slim-style wallets that won't chafe skin and are designed for just this purpose.

- As always in public places, your phone screen and earbuds significantly reduce your Situational Awareness—if you are using both, you're effectively blind and deaf to the world around you. If you're using public transportation in a strange city or any area you're unfamiliar with, or if you're visiting a major tourist destination, do not use your earbuds or your phone unless you're stopped and in a spot that affords you some protection.

- Ensure luggage tags, especially those with PII (personally identifiable information, just think anything that identifies you), are not exposed on public transportation. This is not merely so you can't be easily identified but also so no one can see your address and therefore know where you live while you're away.

- If you're traveling internationally and have just passed through customs and immigration, stop and sort out your passport and identification *before* leaving the airport. If you do it on public transportation or outside, not only are you oblivious to threats because you're distracted, you're basically announcing, "Hey, feel free to grab my passport and make a run for it. I don't mind."

- When traveling with friends or family on public transportation, stand face-to-face so you can watch each other's backs, especially if you have backpacks on or one person is carrying a purse.

- Alternatively, you can stand back-to-back and face away from each other so no one can approach you from behind.

- If you're alone, don't stand with your back to others if you can help it. Where possible, put your back to a window or other vertical surface to keep criminals from having a clear shot at your backpack or being able to shoulder-surf what you're looking at on your phone.

- You can also take off a backpack or hold your purse in your hands or on your lap. If you do, double-wrap straps around your arm.

- Ensure bag or backpack zippers are fully closed and at the top or in another position on your bag/backpack where you can observe them.

- If you're wearing something on your back or think you feel someone digging into a back pants pocket or your pack, back into them. This is an aggressive move and is disruptive. You can always apologize if it's an innocent gesture, but taking action is better than ignoring it.

- When walking with parents, elderly people, or kids, don't lead from the front. Walk behind them so you can observe people approaching them and also to keep an eye on the rear. Most attacks come from behind.

- Use and practice your SDR skills. People-watch via window reflections. Use the glass in subways, trains, and buses.

WEAPONS

Firearms

For the vast majority of people, firearms are overrated, trouble to transport, and legally perilous. Just had to state that upfront. By all means keep a gun in your home or conceal carry in your (US) state if you wish. Weapons can save your life when properly employed, especially in the home. Yet guns, more than any other self-defense tool, can induce a false sense of invulnerability, which means your senses are not fully employed, which means you are not Situationally Aware. And that is what you *don't* want. A firearm as a source of security and confidence also does you no good in Manhattan, Milan, or Mali if you can't take it with you.

This book is designed to keep you safe around the world as well as around the home, and the tools I provide are your best defense. A gun is a last resort. I am certainly not anti-gun. At one time I was among the best combat shooters in the world (everyone where I worked was) and I believe in the practical application of firepower when necessary. But if you need firepower outside of combat, you've probably failed the lessons of this book.

I'm also not a big proponent of concealed carry or the use of firearms in self-defense for all but an exceptional few. Most people, particularly in the US where training requirements are virtually nonexistent, are not qualified or proficient in firearms use. The fact is, most people who own firearms for self-defense rarely, if ever, fire them (these days that includes me). And when they do practice firing them, it is not under the conditions they will experience should they come under attack or witness one. Furthermore, if you shoot someone, you're open to legal prosecution, criminal and civil. In light of all the above, I recommend other forms as replacements for firearms or as first lines of defense for most people. And no child ever killed themselves with a tactical pen or can of Mace.

Tactical Pens

As an alternative to, and improvement upon, firearms I suggest using a tactical pen. These low-cost and very durable pens are exactly that, a working instrument for writing (I prefer and carry a Benchmade brand). Tactical pens are not like other self-defense weapons in that there isn't some secret knife blade to whip out. Rather it has purpose-built hardened construction (often titanium or steel) and size designed to better fit in the hand so you can wield it as a striking weapon against your attacker. They can be taken on trips and are legal for commercial air travel as carry-ons, but when used in self-defense can thwart an attack, and even be lethal.

Without delving into detailed tactics of using one against an attacker (and I always recommend receiving instruction in their use), the best places for striking are the eyes, throat, and head. These are the most shocking places to experience a sharp point, and repeated strikes will dishearten most attackers. Strike as hard as you can, viciously, channeling your inner anger and adrenaline at them for wanting to harm you, until you can break away and then, you guessed it, run like hell.

Tactical pens serve two purposes. The first, as noted above, is as an actual tool you can carry anywhere that has utility value in addition to security. The second is the knowledge you have one. Believing you're protected is half the battle, especially as you learn to project your new image as anything *but* a victim. Regarding tactical pens, I have a saying: "The pen *is* a mighty sword." Brilliant, I know, thank you.

Mace

Mace can be a great weapon, especially for women. It's cheap and can be easily replaced if lost or purchased while away from home. However, if you take trips, especially if you fly a lot, Mace has drawbacks. The first is you can't take it with you on your person through security screening. Laws vary from country to country, but in America you can't carry it onboard and you're only allowed to check a 4 oz. (118 ml) size. Even then, its concentration cannot exceed 2 percent of CS or CN tear gas, the most common active ingredients. Bear sprays, as an alternative, cannot even be checked. Mace is a great defense for use when you move around your local area and in the workplace (be sure to check with your employer, who may have policies about Mace or other items considered weapons, before taking it there).

Any commercial product should have instructions, but if not, there is only one place to apply Mace—the face, particularly the eyes to blind them. Like all weapons it must be immediately available without forethought. If it's buried in a purse or backpack you might as well not have purchased it. As always, as soon as you apply a healthy facial dose (and you're not here to conserve it for the next attack, so empty that baby) your immediate action is to break away and run like hell.

Flashlights

Flashlights are great from a personal defense perspective because you can use them to blind a potential attacker, making it harder for them to get their hands on you, or to introduce a short delay or disruption during an attack, allowing you to escape. It's important to buy LED versions because they're the brightest and most blinding. Small versions fit on key chains, in purses, and in the car. In the home, heavy Maglites (the kind often associated with police) provide multiple use as a means to search for intruders, blind someone so you can escape, or hit them, using it like a club. You can also take a flashlight with you on airplanes as either carry-on or checked baggage.

Knives and Clubs

In general, I don't support carrying knives as a primary tool for self-defense. They're considered (rightfully so) to be offensive weapons by most law enforcement agencies. And you can't take them with you on commercial aircraft. Least desirable of all, they may look menacing but in actuality are difficult to employ if your intent is to disable an attacker. Their best value is their appearance; if you pull a knife it can give the other party pause, which has value in and of itself. But unless you're going for the throat to kill, or the eyes to maim, they won't stop a determined attacker. Of course, if you get training on edged weapons and practice, they can be effective, so I'm not pooh-poohing them. I carry a knife for all backcountry use (they serve multiple purposes) and keep a combat-style blade in my truck. I do have a buddy who successfully defended himself with one in combat, but it was a last resort in a desperate situation, and he was highly trained. You are *not* that person.

Clubs can come in many forms, some intended for self-defense and others merely a convenient conversion. As suggested, a Maglite D-cell works, but as they have limited reach, their value is primarily their weight. In the home, wooden baseball bats are cheap, have solid mass when striking (always aim for the head), and project an appropriate threat to attackers. Many other items can be improvised: 2 x 4 commercial lumber, a stick or cane, a shovel or other garden tool. But like many improvisations, unless the item is at hand when the moment comes, you might as well be armed with a sponge.

A FEW WORDS ON MARTIAL ARTS

As you've learned, this book's purpose is how to avoid a situation. Martial arts, like the weapons and dual-use items above, are outside its purview. However, I'd be remiss if I didn't weigh in on the subject. Martial arts are great preparation and confidence boosters for a fight, should you be trapped. I'd qualify that statement with the reality that most forms and studios do not provide the necessary "real world" situational training or skills that translate into the effective disabling of an attacker. Your goal with this training is first and foremost to escape, not enter into some Bruce Lee fight where you finish off Chuck Norris. Remember your math homework from Rule 6: distance = safety.

However, I do believe martial arts have value because they change your perspective from victim to fighter if nothing else. In the right discipline and with enough practice they can make even the smallest or most timid individual a lethal encounter for the bad guy. In this vein all martial arts training has value to some extent. The type of martial art you choose is important because in reality almost all fights end up on the ground. They never start with two people squaring off the way many forms emphasize (unless you're in a Hollywood movie scene). If you do decide to take one up, I highly recommend Krav Maga for its emphasis on no-holds-barred close-quarters combat and rapid finish.

Calvin Longton spent twenty-four years in the military, first as a Force Recon Marine, then a handful of years as a Green Beret before passing the majority of his career as an Air Force Combat Controller. Before he ever put on a uniform, however, he was already drawn to martial arts and after nearly five decades he's now a 6th-degree Hapkido black belt, 2nd-degree Krav Maga black belt, and 1st-degree Taekwondo black belt among many other disciplines. He's owned and run the Precision Martial Arts training center in Navarre, Florida, for the past nineteen years and also teaches hand-to-hand combatives to the Air Force's most elite and lethal force, Combat Controllers. In short, Master Longton knows what he's talking about.

"I've been doing martial arts since I was sixteen. For the first thirty years I immersed myself in a number of disciplines including Hapkido, Taekwondo, Brazilian Jiu-Jitsu, Muay Thai, and Wing Chun Kung Fu but ultimately came to realize that Krav Maga has the most value in true self-defense. I teach Krav because it's real and allows you to finish the fight quickly. People study other martial arts and can become quite good in forms and grappling, but that's not how real violence happens. Krav has well-thought-out solutions to those life-threatening situations where you face such weapons as knives, handguns, and other real-world threats."

CONCLUSION

Everything in this tool and every means of preparedness requires some form of familiarity, training, and regular practice to be fully implemented. The extent to which you choose the item, train with it, and practice under realistic conditions will determine how they benefit you, which in turn decides (to the extent you need them) the outcome of a particular threat situation. You cannot demand performance from unfamiliar items any more than you might expect to use your car as a getaway vehicle because you own one but never learned how to drive.

A final comment on weapons. No matter what you choose to arm yourself with, and I do recommend owning a tactical pen and flashlight at a minimum, they need to be instantly accessible. Instantly accessible. Did I mention how accessible they need to be? If you can't grab it instinctively at the same time you realize you're under threat, you might as well have saved the money on the purchase, because they won't do you any good if you have to announce, "Time out. Let me just find that mini atomic bomb I keep in here for just such an occasion. Now, where did I put that?"

With that in mind, a good assessment for home placement of weapons is to ask this question: "If someone broke in during the evening or at night, where would I need a club/mace/knife/gun staged so I could grab one without having to take more than two to three steps?" You'll discover that a single item in one spot isn't enough and that you'll require several to avoid having to race to another room to retrieve something. Mixing and matching is also appropriate. Mace in a kitchen drawer and bathroom and a heavy flashlight under a couch cushion, complemented by a baseball bat under the bed, for instance. Use your imagination and spend an afternoon purchasing and placing them. Then, as a final step, practice retrieving them in the dark. You might find it necessary to adjust where you place items. Your home should feel safer already just thinking about it.

TOOL TWO

REDUCING YOUR CRIMINAL TARGET PROFILE

YOU ARE A TRANSMITTER

WHEN WE ASSESS THE DIFFERENT ENVIRONMENTS IN WHICH WE FIND ourselves, it is not always merely the places and people we observe in those environments. You are not separate from your environment. You are one with it, immersed in the same space as the objects, both animate and inanimate. Because of that, you are also transmitting information to the world around you and those in it about who you are, what you are doing, and where you are doing it. And your signal, just like that of any radio, is conveying that information to others who then receive and interpret it. Normally this isn't a problem because it's how we socialize and conduct business. It's when your signal is received by criminals or predators that it becomes problematic.

Predators key in on prey signals, and you don't want to be transmitting signs of vulnerability. In Victoria's case the differences about her transmitted the fact that she was neither Kuwaiti nor Lebanese and therefore something different to her pursuers. That, combined with her status as a lone female, made her worth targeting at a minimum, and possibly worth attacking, for money or rape, and to Victoria at that moment it didn't matter which.

Body Language and Posture

One of the first things to realize about yourself is the way your posture tells others who you are. I'm not suggesting that you change your personality for the sake of safety. Quite the opposite. I want you to become more aware of who you are, but through the eyes of others. And it only truly matters when you're in situations in which you may be vulnerable to predators. Because, aware or not, like it or not, predators are judging you for victim potential and ease of attack. This is particularly true for psychopathic predators who are more likely to victimize strangers, especially those whom they perceive as vulnerable.

A 2018 study of convicted violent psychopaths concluded that gait was how most specifically identify a victim's potential, with the most vulnerable being ones who shifted their weight from side to side in a more pronounced way, "while subjects evaluated as non-vulnerable shifted their weight in a fluid [manner]." Walking slowly and without purpose was also identified as preferable for targeting. An earlier study that focused more on women as targets confirmed that those who "had less-synchronous walks were perceived to be less confident and more vulnerable to sexual assault." All this is to say that the smoother, more confident and purposeful your walk, the less likely you are to appear to be a desirable target. Ted Bundy, the infamous serial killer and rapist, made clear this tendency since he "could tell a victim by the way she walked down the street, the tilt of her head, the manner in which she carried herself."

Yet a third study conducted in 2002 validates that tight clothing, high heels, and other eye-catching attire, including such things as high-end watches and jewelry, will draw attention. All of the findings above are backed by a 2013 study with the following caveat: "Although responsibility for victimization always lies with the perpetrator, our findings have implications for the prevention of future and repeated victimization. Targets who displayed vulnerable body language were more likely to report past histories of victimization, and psychopaths identified these individuals as being more vulnerable to future victimization." I certainly agree that responsibility rests with the perpetrator and that nobody is **ever** "asking for it" but also acknowledge that attire plays a role in targeting by criminals, especially those who are more likely to be violent or sexual predators.

My advice in regard to this topic, as with almost all my advice, goes back to Rules 1 and 2. Choosing what to wear and when is no different than choosing where to go and when. Some situations are simply safer than others, and you are choosing to either increase or decrease your safety odds in the choices you make and your level of awareness. I am not talking solely about attire that may be revealing or sexy, but whatever you're wearing that identifies you as a desirable target. Tourists, particularly Americans in my experience, strolling the streets of London or Rome are prime criminal marks expressly because their attire transmits "American tourist" and therefore pickpockets in Piccadilly or the Colosseum zero in on them. This simple fact makes you, if you're one of them, a more likely target. Don't be. Here's a story.

Dublin, Ireland

My wife and I were in town doing research for another book and sitting outside the beautiful Christ Church Cathedral having just enjoyed fish and chips from Dublin's oldest "chipper," Leo Burdock. It was unseasonably pleasant weather for late October, and the fall crowds were out. I was trying to wipe the last of the chip residue (it's really tasty but let's face it, good fish and chips are a mess) from my hands as we stepped onto the main thoroughfare, when I heard a shout of "Help! Stop him!" from behind us.

I turned to see a woman shouting and dashing into the street. She was pointing in our direction. A twentysomething guy with short black hair and a beard only a college student could think looked good was on a bike peddling furiously our way, a bag dangling from his handlebars. He was by me before I had the chance to clothesline him off his bike. I took a futile step after him, but he was gaining speed by the second and already beyond reach. I turned back to the woman, who had run into the street among the light car traffic.

"Somebody stop him! STOP!!" she frantically repeated. Two things struck me. The first was her attire: tourist garb extraordinaire. But the other thing that left an impression was the way she ran, which I would describe as tentative.

Before we could offer any assistance, a dark blue sedan that could only have been an unmarked police car screeched to a halt and the rear passenger door opened. She pointed past us, shouted "That's him! That's him!" before falling inside and slamming the door. The car raced off after the thief. I don't know which was more impressive, the appearance of the cops within thirty seconds of the crime or their ability to get the woman into the vehicle and underway in about five seconds.

Perhaps it was due to the crisis, but there was something about the way she moved that said "tourist"—in her case German. Were I a criminal, I could see how she'd make an appealing initial mark. Still, I was sorry I didn't get the opportunity to knock the thief in the dirt.

Compounding the problem for all of us as potential targets is the fact that the higher the psychopathic score criminals achieved in these studies, the more accurate they were in judging victims' vulnerabilities. But there are things that help guard against this type of passive targeting. Self-defense training serves as a deterrent. As I mentioned in Tool 1, I am a fan of Krav Maga for its focus on realism and tactics that have nothing to do with fair fights and everything to do with taking maximum advantage of your opponent. This is borne out in a 2018 study (which appeared in a periodical called the *Journal of Interpersonal Violence*, no less) in which the authors, all three professional researchers and psychologists, state, "If psychopaths are picking up on vulnerability expressed through gait and body language, perhaps those cues can be altered as a result of taking a self-defense course, which may decrease one's risk of victimization by adjusting the aspects of body language that suggest vulnerability."

Returning to Victoria's experience in Kuwait, her body language and posture were not what separated her from the throngs of shoppers. She knew how to walk like a local and how, as a born and raised New Yorker, to gesture in a way that transmits, "I'm not a good target." As Victoria puts it, "We talk fast and wave our hands when we do. I think it's in the bagels or something." Regardless of whether that's true about New York bagels, more important, her gait and body language projected confidence. And criminals, especially psychopaths like Ted, don't like that.

ARMED THREATS AND ACTIVE SHOOTERS

North Hollywood, California

THE BANK OF AMERICA BRANCH OPENED RIGHT ON TIME AT 9:00 A.M. Assistant branch manager Juan Villagrana was in charge of the handful of employees of the small branch on Laurel Canyon Boulevard. Customers began to trickle in on the kind of comfortably warm and sunny winter morning only Southern California can produce. Fifteen minutes after opening, Villagrana was startled to see a customer propelled through the door by a giant man in a dark coat and ski mask who was armed with an XM-15 assault rifle fitted with a hundred-round drum magazine. As the hostage was pushed inside, a second and smaller masked gunman, also armed with an assault rifle, appeared.

The first robber pushed the hostage out of the way, swearing, fired a sustained burst into the ceiling, and announced, "This is a holdup. Everybody get down on the floor. Close your eyes and don't look." He strutted across the lobby as most everyone dropped to the ground, delivering a warning as he went: "Keep your heads down! If you move, I'll kill you!" Customer Mildred Nolte was stunned, trying to figure out what was happening, when the larger robber smashed her in the head with his fist, knocking her to the ground. "I guess

I didn't move fast enough," recalled the then seventy-nine-year-old retiree in a later interview.

The lead robber then turned his attention on Enrique Figueroa, the thirty-two-year-old uniformed security guard, who had only too quickly realized what was going on and had already dropped to the floor. A moment later he found a boot on his head accompanied by the muzzle of the assault rifle shoved against his neck and an instruction, "When I tell you, I want you to move all these people into the vault."

Meanwhile, the second robber fired his weapon into the vault's teller access doors, trying to break them open. When that failed, he confronted Villagrana, striking him in the head with the butt of his rifle and demanding that he open it. The manager took a set of keys off another employee and did as instructed. When the gunman handed him a large nylon gear bag, he began filling it from the money boxes inside. But they were all small bills, further infuriating the gunman, who then opened fire on the remaining boxes and yelled at the manager, "You have millions. Where's the ATM money?" The manager didn't have the ability to open the ATMs, explained Villagrana, which resulted in another fusillade of bullets into the ATM machines, some of which ricocheted back, wounding Villagrana. The first robber then gave the signal for Figueroa, the security guard, to bring the customers and employees into the vault, where they were left untied, and alone, though a few were injured.

Eight minutes after entering, the two men, clad in body armor and dragging the gear bag, walked out of the bank and into one of the most notorious shootouts in US law enforcement history.

For the patrons and employees, they were simply in the wrong place at the wrong time. Confronted with armed robbers who began firing the moment they were inside the bank, each person asked themselves this question in one form or another: "What do I do?" In their circumstances, and because of the risk of being shot by the robbers (who were both high on phenobarbital), the answer every person arrived at that morning was to either take cover or comply as directed.

But should you find yourself inside that bank, the question "What should I do?" isn't the first question to ask yourself in a situation like this one. Your first question should actually be, "Who am I?" Because the answer to that question tells you if you are in the wrong place at the wrong time or *you* are the target. For the bank employees and customers, it's the former.

For responding law enforcement officers outside the bank, the question "Who am I?" is also valid. It's the answer that is different. Every officer's answer is "I am a target," and so for the police officers assembling outside, the two shooters were no longer robbers but assassins. The shooters' goal after exiting the bank, while never stated, was to kill officers wherever they stood. In the end, both assailants died by gunfire, the first by his own hand when he saw no chance of escape, the second as a result of extensive wounds from police fire.

The North Hollywood bank robbery provides a case study of both types of active shooter situations you can find yourself in: Either it's the wrong place at the wrong time, or you are the intended target.

WHAT ARE THE ODDS?

Active shootings make headlines nearly every day in Europe (including the United Kingdom) and North America. In the United States, where I live and spend most of my time, the sense is that it's pervasive if not absolutely epidemic.

In 2019 there were 434 mass shootings in America.[9] Expressed in daily terms, that's 1.19 mass shootings per day. The US has 331 million people who own a staggering 393 million civilian firearms, for a human-to-weapon ratio of 1.2 firearms per citizen. Put another way, Americans comprise 4 percent of the world's population but 46 percent of its private firearms ownership. Our worldwide lead in this statistic is only increasing.

The root causes of the mass shooting problem in America are many and hotly debated, and I am not here to weigh in on the argument. Except to say, any country that exceeds its population in weapons should not be surprised that incidents involving them continue to rise. If we had 331 million people and 393 million dogs (only about 20 percent of us own dogs, for a total of approximately 90 million), no one would be stunned at a disproportionate number of dog bites in this country compared to other nations. In Europe, mass shootings are less sensationalized but still more frequent now than at any time in history. In select years other countries (Norway in 2011 and France in 2015 for instance) have exceeded the US in mass shooting fatality ratios, but these anomalies are due to horrific attacks with outsized nationwide impact on less populated countries and nowhere near what the US experiences daily year in and year out.

As someone who made my living with one for three decades, I am not anti-firearm, but I do find the ease with which guns can be acquired, in my country at least, disturbing. Of the 393 million weapons in the United States only approximately 1 million are registered, meaning the vast majority can move around at will. It seems inevitable that with so many weapons in circulation they will find their way into violence. I suppose the upside is that any country considering an invasion should think that plan over carefully since

---

9   Mass shootings here are defined as four or more victims in a single incident, which may include the perpetrators.

the US civilian arsenal is three times the size of all foreign military small arms combined.

So how dangerous was it really for you as a civilian in 2019? Statistically speaking, using the numbers above, the odds of you being killed are about 1 in 153,000 in a given year in the United States.[10] I was surprised at the number because I expected it to be closer to the probability of being struck by lightning (1 in 1.2 million in a given year according to the National Weather Service). This makes you roughly eight times more likely to be involved in a mass shooting than a lightning strike. Still, the odds of you encountering one in your lifetime are low.

However, while the odds of being directly involved in a mass shooting are low, it is an extremely high-consequence event that can lead to a lifetime of post-traumatic stress or PTSD. As with everything else in this book, you improve your odds of emerging safely by best understanding what is actually happening, and that is determined by asking one simple question.

UNDERSTANDING WHO YOU ARE IN A SHOOTING CRISIS

Who am I in an armed threat/active shooter situation? The answer is you are only ever in one of two categories. You are either **in the wrong place at the wrong time**, such as making a deposit at 9:15 a.m. in

---

10   This statistic neglects the number of shootings and victims that aren't classified as mass. The true number of firearm victims in the US is much higher. My review of all 434 mass shootings in the US that year revealed that domestic situations where the shooter knew the victims were quite common and had no extremist connection. Furthermore, these mass shooting statistics do not include numbers for single or dual murder victims. Those numbers are truly staggering. Regardless of your opinion on gun violence, the fact is you're many times more likely to be shot by someone you know than an extremist of any particular religious or political bent.

the lobby of the North Hollywood Bank of America on February 28, 1997. In this case you are incidental to the perpetrators' objectives and therefore you are *not* the intended target.

Or you are **the target**, such as a synagogue goer at the Tree of Life Jewish center in Pittsburgh, Pennsylvania, on October 27, 2018; a patron of Pulse nightclub in Orlando, Florida, on June 12, 2016; or a student/faculty member of Columbine High School on April 20, 1999. In these instances, the shooter or shooters have come to that location specifically to kill, and therefore *you* are the target.

In the former it doesn't matter your race, gender, sexual orientation, or religion because your SA and Intuition tell you that the perpetrators are here for money, not you. In the latter instances it is easy to deduce that you and those around you are the target, quite likely *because* of your race, gender, sexual orientation, status, membership (through enrollment or employment, etc.), or religion.

So the more refined question you need to ask as soon as you hear gunshots or believe you're in a potential situation where someone is armed and possibly killing people is: **Am I in the wrong place at the wrong time or am I the target?**

The answer to that single question determines what you need to do next. It's important to answer it quickly because you need to act rapidly and appropriately if you are to improve your odds of escape. And escape is the best way of resolving your problem. Fortunately, everything goes right back to your six rules, beginning with SA and Intuition. If you are asking the "who am I" question, you already know the answer to Rule 3 because you definitely have a problem. Now you need to develop a plan (Rule 4) and act (Rule 5), and you need to do both rapidly because time is always going to be of essential importance.

WRONG PLACE, WRONG TIME

There is no calculator that can provide a statistic on when and where is the wrong place and wrong time. The fact is it could be just about anywhere: a convenience store, grocery store, restaurant, any theater or park. If you make the determination that you're simply an unfortunate combination of timing and location, your first plan should be to escape. Flee. Run like hell. Call it what you will, but in those first few seconds of realization, if you think you can make it out the door or out of the area, do it. Think of our hero Hector from the Shop an' Spend.

Regardless of the structure or environment you find yourself in when you make your decision to run for your life, don't hesitate. The moment you make that decision, you are in fact implementing Rule 5, Act Decisively. And when you run, run as fast as you can. Run like hell. Move side to side or serpentine as you run. Moving targets, despite every Hollywood film you've ever seen, are nearly impossible to hit. And when you get a safe distance, keep moving, blocks if necessary, miles are better still. If you have a car parked in the vicinity of the attack, leave it behind. You can always come back for it. As soon as you're safe, phone the police. Let them know you were involved because your information as an insider will be invaluable (as opposed to others calling in who were not).

There are places where escaping simply isn't possible, such as the North Hollywood bank robbery. Banks only have one door for a reason, but for a bystander that can make it a dead-end trap. In these cases, your course of action is to evade the shooter. Dodge behind the nearest counter or other object that will obstruct the shooter's view of you if possible, preferably one that affords some ballistic protection. In the military, anything that protects you from enemy observation and fire is known as defilade, but that's merely cover and concealment by another name.

By evading, you remain out of their line of sight and therefore less likely to be selected as a hostage or shield or for any of a number of other undesirable uses. You're trying to be invisible at this point. If you can make it into other rooms or sections of the building, do so. Which is why I refer to it as evading and not hiding. The word "hide" is passive and, like the game hide and seek, lends itself mentally to finding one spot and waiting until you're found. But you don't want to be discovered. So think of evading, an active verb, continuing to search for a way out or another and better place to evade the shooter.

There is also safety in numbers. Take others with you or join them. Just like Hector in the Shop an' Spend, you might be able to alter the outcome. If not for yourself then for others. An alternative is a bolt-hole hiding spot you absolutely know the shooter can't find. If you're forced to hunker down, no matter where you go, stay put longer than you think necessary. Your first action once you stop is, should you have a phone on you, to silence all notifications because any noise is bad. Likewise, for making and receiving calls. Texts are better. Text someone where you are and the details as you understand them and have them phone the police.

Every decision you make in a shooter crisis is a personal choice. You may not have control of the situation. However, by making active choices you gain back some influence over the outcome. When escaping or evading aren't options, you may find yourself faced with interacting with the shooter. Remember, in **wrong place/wrong time** they aren't after you. Should you be forced to comply, there are a few things to keep in mind. First, now is not the time to play Bruce Willis in *Die Hard*. It is best not to be defiant in posture or eye contact, in fact avoiding eye contact is preferable. If they want you to do something, do only what is asked. If you have to move around with them or at their direction, you should continually be searching for places that offer cover should shooting start (with the police or others), because you'll want to immediately go to ground when it does, and anything that affords you protection may make all the difference.

Should you find yourself outdoors or in the open in a wrong place/wrong time scenario, you still need to make choices regarding escaping or evading. It's going to be scary, certainly, but you'll likely instinctively know where the shooting is coming from. Take an instant to determine that. Veteran LAPD Detective Hutch was a first responder during the North Hollywood bank robbery, where he was responsible for guiding numerous civilians to safety during the sustained gunfight (he's also married to Detective Starsky). The Bank of America shootout is not his only experience with armed threats and robbers, and his decades of expertise can be distilled into a simple decision and action: "Run. And as soon as you can, run perpendicular to the direction of fire because bullets travel a long way. One other thing, action, any action [on your part] is better than inaction or letting them control your fate."

YOU AS THE TARGET

Columbine, Colorado

On the morning of April 20, 1999, just before 11:30 a.m., two members of Columbine High School arrived armed with assault rifles, shotguns, and homemade bombs. Their intent was to kill as many people at the school as possible, though they had strongest resentment against those they considered to be "jocks." They announced their intentions as they left the student parking lot by shooting two students enjoying lunch outside, killing one instantly and severely wounding the other. Once inside, they began shooting indiscriminately in the hallways. In the cafeteria a short distance away, teacher and coach Dave Sanders heard the gunfire, recognized it for what it was, and began warning students, who were all eating lunch at that time. Moments later the two killers entered the cafeteria and begin spraying fire. Both were then distracted by student gawkers observing the unfolding melee from the school's soccer field, so they unleashed bullets at the soccer crowd through the cafeteria's windows.

Sanders, thinking quickly, herded a group upstairs away from the killers and ushered them into a science lab, but was shot in the course of his heroic defense. Both killers then proceeded to the library on the second floor where fifty-six students and teachers had taken refuge. Inside, the two began asking jocks to stand up and identify themselves. None did.

Through the library windows the killers noticed police evacuating students and shot out the glass in that direction. When the police returned fire, both teens withdrew and focused their attention inside, with one repeating his demand that jocks stand up. When no one did, he announced, "Fine, I'll just start shooting." They proceeded to taunt and shoot a number of students, killing several. One student, lying in the blood of a victim, feigned death. Another hostage was let go because he was an acquaintance of one of the attackers. The killers then decided to depart, but before leaving the library, one shot under a nearby table at three hostages, one of whom, a shy fifteen-year-old named Daniel Mauser, either pushed a chair at the shooter or tried to grab his leg (accounts vary), likely in the attempt to disrupt his actions. He was shot in the head at point-blank range and died. Shooting randomly under another table on the way out, they wounded two, killed what turned out to be their final victim, and departed. Without waiting to see if the killers might return, the twenty-nine uninjured and ten injured survivors evacuated the library through an emergency exit.

The killers walked the school for approximately twenty more minutes trying to set off bombs they'd placed and taunting those suspected to be hiding in spots such as restrooms, eventually working their way back to the empty library (fully evacuated except for two injured students who'd been left behind). There, after exchanging some fire with police outside, the two cowards shot themselves.

A few lessons of value in considering your own decisions and actions in the Columbine shooting scenario, should you have been there:

1. The first two victims, sitting outside eating lunch together, had no chance. Nothing indicated they were about to be shot, even though one of the killers had thrown an improvised pipe bomb in the parking lot that only partially exploded a moment beforehand. It was later stated by the one surviving lunch victim and other witnesses that they thought the bomb was a prank. It's possible that the two could have immediately run away, but that's a difficult argument to make as it takes time to process and decide against an unannounced threat. Tragically, both outdoor diners never even knew they were under threat.

2. In the cafeteria after the initial shooting was heard, faculty member Dave Sanders's quick thinking saved a number of lives when he recognized a momentary gap in the murderers' attention. His decisive actions were sound choices. If you see a gap, take it.

3. When the killers saw gawkers through the cafeteria windows, they engaged them with gunfire. While none of the gawkers were hit, their very presence rubbernecking was a foolish and typical response to an attack such as this. Don't be a gawker. Leave.

4. In the initial library confrontation, when the killers demanded that jocks stand up, none did. Some, easily identified by distinctive shirts and hats bearing the school's logo, were even shielded or masked by others. Both actions were good and brave choices. Complying or singling yourself out is unlikely to save anyone, least of all yourself. And if you have the chance to hide someone who is being targeted, you're taking a brave and very humane stance.

5. The student who feigned death by lying in the blood of another victim made a sound choice. He couldn't flee (none could at this point) and he couldn't hide because moving would draw attention to himself. Instead, he courageously improvised, instinctively believing that the killer, occupied by many thoughts and targets, would pass him by. And he was correct.

6. The only person to directly confront the killers physically was young Daniel Mauser. It's impossible to say what his real intention was. He probably believed it would at least disrupt the killer. So, defiant or courageous. However, if he thought that he was about to die or that by disrupting the killer he was saving someone else, he should have physically and aggressively attacked his killer. My book is not designed to provide

the training or expertise to launch such an attack, but I'll say this: Your life depends on the ferocity and the clarity of your action in that fraction of a second. And you should use both as if disabling or killing the person in front of you is the only thing that matters in your life. Because it is. But once a single person acts (just as in the Shop an' Spend case) others can and often will join in. The tide against killers like these can be turned in those precious seconds.

7. As soon as the killers left the library, the remaining hostages immediately fled the scene. Absolutely the correct action to take, and further reinforced by the fact that the two killers returned there to end their lives. There's little doubt that before doing so they would have killed more hostages.

Being the target isn't a statement about who you are. Your race, gender, orientation, profession, or religion are not the categorization you should be thinking about in your crisis. It is rather, What place am I in and how does the killer see it and therefore by extension me? Sometimes this is quite straightforward. If you're inside the Pittsburgh synagogue (or any place of worship) and hear shouts of fear and gunshots, you needn't rely on your Intuition, you know you're a target just by being inside, whether you're Jewish or not. The same is true for school shootings like Columbine. In a nightclub like Pulse it's possible you've stumbled into a robbery or perhaps a personal vendetta or even a gang fight, making it a bit harder to categorize. But choose you must.

Your first course of action remains the same as in a wrong place/

wrong time situation: Escape, run for it if at all possible. And if you make it to safety, don't stop. Don't gawk. As always, keep going beyond where you might initially feel safe.

If you can't escape, begin evading, even if there are few options. If you're at your place of work you'll be more familiar with possibilities (see next section); if not you will be forced to make quite rapid choices. In the latter case, evade as far from the shooting as possible. For example, at Columbine, some students and faculty made for the gymnasium initially. Going as a group has advantages. Silencing your phone becomes imperative, just as in a wrong place/wrong time situation. Any noise is bad, and a ringing phone or your own voice during a call could give you away. Use texts if you're unsure where the killers are or what's happening, and have someone else contact the police and tell people where you are and what the situation is. In this type of shooting scenario you may be trapped for an extended period, and it'll pay to conserve battery power. If you think this might be the case, let people know you could be communicating sparingly. But it's still a two-way communication, and you can use your phone to learn not only what's going on but whether, if the situation changes, you might possibly have an opportunity to escape, because that should always remain at the forefront of your mind.

If you're confronted, and you believe your life is about to end, your last course is to defend yourself. And you should be prepared for this possibility beforehand if you want your chances to be as good as possible. Just as in any situation, taking decisive action (Rule 5) is likely the best chance you have for a positive outcome. Gouge eyes, punch or kick knees and groins (your active shooter is almost certainly male). Bash on their head and face, especially the nose, which is sensitive and causes the eyes to tear up. And if they go down, don't stop. No fair fighting required; it's undeserved.

It's possible you won't make it, just as Daniel Mauser didn't. But in my opinion and that of other experts, you're better off taking the fight to the bad guys and letting them know you won't go quietly into that dark night. The world always needs more true heroes, and acting out of necessity, as you've learned, is the very definition of the word. My only wish here is that you are never afforded the opportunity.

Police officer A. J. DeAndrea was a SWAT leader during the 1999 Columbine shooting and then again at another lone-gunman high school shooting in Platte Canyon, Colorado, in 2006. There he was a mere four feet from the killer when that coward was taken down. DeAndrea has since become an international expert on active shooters. However, his experience and expertise are not confined to the response side. In November 2018 his daughter was enjoying an evening of country-western dancing at the Borderline Bar and Grill in Thousand Oaks, California, when a shooter entered the club and opened fire, ultimately killing twelve. Because she'd grown up her father's daughter, she was prepared. Realizing she couldn't escape, she, along with a few patrons and a bartender, evaded by climbing into the bar's attic. All survived. His nephew survived yet another high school shooter and escaped, in this case by literally running for his life.

The DeAndrea family's direct involvement with this many active shooters is so statistically improbable as to be incalculable. My recommendation to him when we spoke was that he consider investment in lottery tickets for retirement, because if anyone can beat those odds, it's him. He consistently emphasized the need to continually and actively think, should you be involved with a shooter. This is manifested in the maxim: Escape, evade, and defend. And that until a police response can assist you, you are on your own and therefore you must take ownership. "The decisions you make are literally between life and death. If you've prepared your mind. If you own your responsibility in a critical event. In that one defining moment of your life you have a better chance of coming out okay and continuing on with your life."

WHERE YOU WORK

One place you should definitely be prepared is at your place of work. Ask questions. What kind of shooter would appear at the place where you spend most of your waking hours? Do you work in the wrong place or are you and your coworkers the likely targets? How would a shooter enter your workplace? You should absolutely know your alternate exits to escape or evade and also places of refuge. By knowing this, you can even help your employer be better prepared for an attack.

Identify your alternate exits. Have two if possible and identify them as 1 and 2. This is so you can automatically and without thinking go to emergency exit 1. You only divert to 2 if your primary option is either blocked or you think it's riskier.

Identify places to hide. Consider their attributes to avoid discovery. Restrooms are not best choices. Dead ends are less desirable for obvious reasons but can be acceptable if they're obscured or difficult to find. Better are locations that might allow you to make your bid for freedom and safety if the shooter comes in from one end. Also consider the location's ability to withstand bullet fire. Know that standard interior office-building walls do not stop bullets, but bricks and cinder block work well. Furniture, cases of paper in sufficient quantities (believe it or not), machinery, and office equipment are good alternatives ballistically.

If you're responsible for others or a business leader, taking some time to prepare your buildings and people is a minimal time investment for a potentially very high preventative safety value. You can contact your local police department for help with this.

—

CONCLUSION

I realize active shooters and the oft-associated extremism that spawns some of them are sensitive topics. My hope in covering this subject is to provide simple decisions and actions for you in the unfortunate and highly unlikely event you should find yourself under fire. The most important first step in a shooter situation is to rapidly determine whether you are the target or just in the wrong place. When you know that, you'll be able to take the appropriate action.

The two cases I selected to highlight are representative of the two categories of shooting crisis. Both were also precedent-setting. The North Hollywood robbery set in motion much of law enforcement's greater use of military weapons and tactics that remain prevalent today. The Columbine shooting led an unfortunate trend. Through individuals' stories and actions from both of these highlighted tragedies you can see where they made a difference or, should you find yourself in their shoes, where you could make a different choice. But these two cases are also examples of extreme conditions and outcomes. Should you somehow find yourself involved in an active shooter situation, it's statistically likely the killer's motivations are connected to the victim (whether yourself or someone else in your vicinity) personally. That doesn't make it better, but knowing that could be advantageous.

Some of the advice in this chapter may seem like statements of the obvious, but nonetheless, or perhaps because of that, it's important to think through and consider these situations beforehand. That's so your response becomes automatic when the crisis strikes, precisely when it's too late to *start* thinking about what you should do. You need to do it.

Nothing I've shared here can guarantee an outcome any more than any combat outcome can be determined with certainty. It's simply not possible to factor in variables such as the location, the shooter's intent and abilities, and even your own actions. But I strongly recommend you make the decision about what to do for yourself. You're taking a chance, of course, but better that than allowing the choice to be the shooter's. Don't leave your fate in the hands of a killer.

TOOL FOUR

REDUCING YOUR PERSONAL INFORMATION FOOTPRINT

PROTECTING THE SLICES OF YOUR PERSONAL PIE

PII, PRONOUNCED EITHER "PEA, EYE, EYE" OR "PIE" (DEPENDING ON whether you're a computer geek or common human), is a broad term that refers to personal information that can either identify who you are or be associated with you. It's a sensitive subject for experts who routinely argue over exactly what it means, which has led to transatlantic friction between America and the European Union (as if either side needs an excuse to argue). In the US, the National Institute of Standards and Technology defines PII as anything that can be used to trace your identity (Social Security numbers, date and place of birth, etc.) and any information that can be linked to you such as your employer or financial and medical records. In the EU they eschew PII, preferring the term "personal information" and using it more broadly, so that something as simple as your internet IP address is considered sensitive. What matters when speaking with the authorities is simply understanding that in America "PII" is the common term and in Europe it's "personal information."

To me and you for purposes of personal safety, PII is simply any information that can be used to identify who you are, find you, and then target you.[11] Think of it this way: If it can be used to identify who you are and/or where to find you at a specific time, it's important to protect. After all, you wouldn't serve up a slice of personal "pie" to Ted Bundy. So don't give one to strangers.

You can also think of your PII as a personal information footprint along the lines of your carbon footprint, and your goal should be to reduce it or keep it as small as possible. Your personal information footprint consists of the actions you take that put your PII (whether it's identification you carry on your person or the data available online) out in the world on a daily basis. Just as reducing your carbon footprint means taking some small but deliberate actions to help the environment, reducing your personal information footprint can help you reduce personal safety risk.

GENERAL RULES FOR INFORMATION PROTECTION

Your personal information vulnerabilities fall into roughly three categories. The first is physical: things people can see or steal that are tangible, such as wallets, proximity reader cards (for building access), your phone or laptop/tablet. The second is device vulnerabilities where your PII is contained, such as hackers accessing your phone or computer when you're using unsecured networks and the like. These first two categories are what can be stolen from you to be used in further theft or for targeting you personally. The final

---

11 Such crimes as tax ID or Social Security fraud and other impersonation-type offenses are outside the scope of this book. They will, however, continue to increase in frequency and severity around the world and I encourage you to spend time considering and investing in protecting that information as well. But it starts with protecting your PII.

vulnerability category is actually a gift from you to ne'er-do-wells everywhere, it is...drumroll...information you freely share with the world. I say it's a gift because you are giving the information away, they're not taking it from you. And it's a gift that keeps on giving because once it's online and out in the world, like nuclear waste or plastic, it's forever. This information is completely legal for others to use in targeting you. Think about that.

Physical Vulnerabilities

Protecting your information and electronics starts with Rule 1, Be Situationally Aware. By paying attention to your surroundings, instead of your phone screen or music, you will prevent criminals and creeps from over-the-shouldering you on trains, buses, planes, and in coffee shops. It's the easiest and least sophisticated means by which to capture personal information from targets. This is particularly true if you're using online banking, social media, or anything that displays your personal information. Be aware of which direction your screen is pointing, and if you're in a crowded space such as a subway or busy street, try to keep your screen as close to your body as possible if you have to look at your phone at all. If you're lazy, you can expect to get compromised and you'll never even know.

Watch what you're displaying outside your clothing. Lanyards for company badges are a dead giveaway, and certainly should not be combined with such things as credit cards or driver's licenses. Sitting in a restaurant or shopping at the grocery store, for instance, with your company badge on display and your driver's license on the other side because it was convenient to put them both in the same badge holder is broadcasting who you are, where you work, and your home address. Having a lunch meeting in a busy and popular café one day, I captured photos of these things in less than four seconds. That's right, *less* than four seconds.

For the close-up of her license I simply hit zoom and snapped again. The young lady has no idea her information was captured (and safely masked because this book is about the good guys) in the time it took for her to have a bite of sandwich alongside her two oblivious companions. I have another snap of the reverse side of her lanyard, which revealed a proximity reader from her employer. Furthermore, the photos aren't even illegal, merely snapshots in a public place. Her same information could be captured on CCTV too, and anyone viewing it there could also incorporate facial recognition into their profile. As I watched the happy trio stroll out to her car and return to their employer (whom I was also able to identify) I noted the final piece of information: make, model, color, and license plate.

Device Vulnerabilities

Mobile devices such as your smartphone or tablet have effectively replaced desktop computers in today's world, yet mobile device security is often overlooked in day-to-day life. Ignoring that nagging "system update available" notification, for example, can leave your cell phone or iPad vulnerable to unauthorized access to sensitive data, data loss, and identity theft. While there's no guarantee you will never experience any type of attack or that there is a way to prevent absolutely every type of attack imaginable, there are basic security practices you can, and should, follow to keep your device and your data as secure as possible.

- Set a lock on your device. Simply having a swipe unlock leaves your phone wide open to anyone who steals it or finds it if it's lost. It's easy to remember a four-digit PIN or a pattern lock. I use 1234 so don't take that because it's already spoken for. Just kidding. Don't you use that or the worse alternative 0000, make it more complex. It can make a huge difference in thwarting unauthorized access to all your information on your phone. Some of you may be thinking, "Oh, I don't do much on my phone except text," but consider this—if a thief gains access to your phone, they gain access to all your contacts and *their* information, not just yours. If you have a Ring doorbell camera (or a similar device from any number of home security vendors), you'll have the app on your phone and likely set to stay logged in. The thief can open the app and see your home address, which could lead them directly to your door. Not something any of us would want. Lock your phone.

- Smartphones can be configured to automatically perform a factory reset, wiping all of your data, after a number of incorrect unlock attempts. If your data is backed up to the cloud, and it should be, you won't lose anything and the thief gains nothing.

- Keep your device updated. While updates tackle things such as bugs and performance issues, the most crucial patches are security related. Whenever you see a notification that there is an update available, make sure you don't ignore it or put it off.

- Use multifactor authentication (MFA) whenever possible. Two-factor authentication is helpful and better than nothing. Both simply add additional steps to the login process, such as sending you a code and using your fingerprint to authenticate you before you're allowed full access to your account. Always use them.

- Be careful what you install on your device. There are many apps out there that have hidden spyware, malware, and the like and that are intended to steal your data. That's right, their reason for existing is not to entertain you by destroying bits of colorful candy, but to capture your information and sell it. Any device you use for online banking or anything that uses sensitive data should be kept clear of apps you're not sure of. Just because it's in the Google Play store doesn't mean it's fully secure. Apple and Google do a good job of vetting and scanning apps, but they can't catch everything. Many apps have been pulled for embedded malware, spyware, and other invasive code. You can further mitigate security and privacy risks by regularly reviewing app permissions and ensuring they only have access to features they need—this can be done in device settings under Privacy. Bottom line—just use common sense with apps. You don't need your fun game that badly. And if you do, install it on something else that isn't used for sensitive things like banking. Otherwise you're gambling with your entire checking account.

- Ensure the Find My iPhone or Find My Device functions are active in case your device is stolen or lost. These programs provide a way to geolocate the device, remotely lock it, and erase the device's data. This can be found under the settings tab on almost every phone manufactured.

- Use a password manager or ensure you are using complex passwords. I know it can seem daunting to try and remember a long string of letters, numbers, and characters, but the more complex you make them, the harder they are to guess. If you can make a pattern or use an acronym that makes personal sense to you and no one else, it can be easy to add a significant level of security to your phone.

- Don't reuse the same passwords for everything. Also, change them regularly. I'm sure you've seen articles about data breaches at big companies, such as the Equifax hack, that expose the user data of millions of people. This information is then available to those who will try to access bank accounts, open credit card accounts, and initiate other types of activities that can cause serious financial damage. One of the best ways to fight this is to regularly change passwords, particularly for online banking, and make them complex, or use a reputable password manager to provide highly complex passwords that can be easily and quickly changed.

- Don't check the "stay logged in" type boxes on apps that provide access to your personal data. Most banking apps will automatically log you out after a certain amount of time. However, apps like Amazon Shopping will keep you logged in, and if your phone is stolen or accessed by someone, you've just given them all they need for their next Christmas to be Merry. Screw that, Ebenezer.

- Back up your data daily. Whether you're an Android or an Apple user, there are built-in backup functions that should be enabled from the first time you use the device. You can choose what gets backed up, but at a minimum you should be backing up your contacts and any other critical files daily. Many service providers such as Verizon, Google, and

Microsoft offer cloud backup, which should be your first choice. If you opt for only saving your data to your device and it gets stolen, everything will be lost.

Two Other Specific Vulnerabilities

Unsecured Wi-Fi networks: Avoid connecting to them. Criminals can exploit public Wi-Fis to steal your personal information, such as emails, photos, contact information, passwords, sensitive documents, and banking information. Using a virtual private network (VPN) is recommended to reduce the risk. A VPN app creates an encrypted "tunnel" between your device and a remote server, protecting your data from snooping bad guys. If you're using your phone to check your bank balance or pay bills on the subway or in a coffee shop, for example, a VPN provides a layer of safety that will help keep your data out of the wrong hands.

Electronic Entry Keys: Electronic hotel room keys are your personal gift card to criminals and rapists. Leaving the extra card on the hotel room counter invites your room cleaner to swap it and sell it and you'd never know. To capture the data on it requires a scanner, so there's a bit of sophistication involved, but more people have these than you realize, and they don't own one so they can put flowers in your hotel room. Any swiped or replicated key can then be used by someone else to enter while you're asleep or to rifle through your belongings when you're out. Foreign intelligence services do this regularly and in more countries than you might think. The foreign officers who do this kind of work are not James Bond and are just as likely to sell information about you gleaned from access to your room (such as from your laptop) as they are to put it in their national database for "security" reasons.

SOCIAL MEDIA PROTOCOLS

Social media platforms are ubiquitous, they are an integral part of our online lives. They are a great way to stay in touch with friends and family and connect to the world. But remember, this is the one area in your life where you are voluntarily giving your information to others, nobody's stealing it. I can tell you that when targeting terrorists and even enemy combatants, one of the best tools for locating them is social media. You unwittingly—or worse, willingly—deliver a treasure trove of information for bad guys to figure out who you are, where you live, the places you frequent, when you're home, and who your family and friends may be. Well done! However, there are simple rules to follow when on social media to thwart those who would do you or your loved ones harm.

- Privacy and security settings on social media platforms exist for a reason. Make sure you're limiting who can see your profile and what you're posting. Use strong passwords for your social media accounts and change them regularly.

- Pay attention to requests to follow you or friend you and only accept requests from those you feel are legitimate. Some people accept any and all requests that come their way. Criminals and stalkers use this to their advantage, sometimes masked as people you may already be connected to.

- Always be careful with what you're posting. Remember, what goes online, stays online forever.

- When going on a trip, whether short or long in duration, for business or pleasure, don't post about it until you've returned. Do not post destinations and dates in advance. They make you a target for stalkers and sophisticated criminals when away from home. They make your house or apartment vulnerable to robbery and leave those who stayed behind vulnerable to home invasions. There are forums for information, usually aggregated from social media where people unwisely share their travel plans before they leave, readily available on the dark web where thieves can look to see who might be gone on vacation or even an overnight trip, making your home easy pickings for theft. No kidding, they can search by geographic location to identify targets, resulting in "Hey, Mr. and Mrs. Smith are gone till Friday. Let's roll!"

- Make sure you've disabled location tagging on your platform. This ensures your posts and images aren't tagged with your location. It also requires you to take a few steps in settings because your social media provider likes to know where you are, the better to sell your information to other vendors. Just what you always wanted!

- Patterns of life. If you visit the same pub, café, coffee shop and post about it daily, you're creating a target profile. Vary your routines so you're not predictable.

CONCLUSION

When considering your PII, what matters most are two things. The first is consistency in what you share and more important what you don't. When you put a piece of critical information out into the cyber world, such as your address, birthdate, place of employment, it's there forever. Never share more than you're willing to give to Ted Bundy . . . and he only needs to find your address once.

The second is unpredictability. Or stated another way, not sharing your patterns of life with the entire world. By letting everyone know what time you arrive at work or home, where you get coffee every day at 10:00 a.m., or where you and your friends meet for drinks after work, you're inviting Ted along too.

DIGITAL TO THREE-DIMENSIONAL DATING

YOU'VE MET SOMEONE, AN INTRIGUING GUY OR GIRL. AND BECAUSE you're savvy and also read Tool 4, you haven't done anything foolish or given away any PII. And also, their name isn't Ted. So it's now time to meet in 3D, a no-kidding opportunity to see if this is the one, or at least the one right now. Because you've read this book you're armed with rules and perhaps Mace or a tactical pen. Here are some tips on getting in and getting out alive. Hopefully you've chosen well and are in for something more fun than just survival, but just in case:

Dinner, coffee, or cocktails, where to and how to do it? If you've read the book thus far, this is an easy decision to make for a first date. You're looking for, or agreeing to, somewhere familiar to you. If they suggest someplace you don't know, counter with "I know this great _____ [fill in the blank]. You'll love it." It also needs to be well lit (you're not looking for the romantic spot to propose or be proposed to), well populated with other patrons for obvious reasons, and have open approaches and departures so you can't be followed back to your metro stop/car/lair. If you met this person online or via an app, don't share additional PII such as your phone number or home address. Pick a spot and time and use the app as backup. If they're still worried about the ability to link up without it, remind them that humans made plans this way for centuries before iPhones and Tinder. But you know all this.

What to do? If that first date is something different than a simple drink or meal, it still needs to be an activity or event where other people are present or that has public exposure. Structured activities are ideal. A climbing gym if you're sporty. Cooking classes or other instructions are interactive and provide defined beginning and ending times. Sporting events or concerts work for meeting publicly. Avoid remote activities such as hiking into the Australian outback, save them for when you know the person better. I recommend sky-diving, but then I would.

Communication. This isn't about how to talk to the other gender or person, you're on your own there. The communication I'm talking about is with your safety net (friends, your mom, a coworker, neighbors). The critical information you need to share is captured in four "Ws": *Who* you're going with (provide a name, phone number, or the contact method you used to set the date). *What* you plan to do. *Where* you plan to do it. *When* you plan to return. On your date, casually mention that your friend, mom, special ops buddy, or FBI agent neighbor thought this date was a great idea when you told them who, what, when, and where.

Another form of communication if you're meeting for drinks is to show up early and tell your bartender or waiter you're on a first date. This was shared with me by a savvy New Yorker and veteran of the dating wars who also happened to be a bartender. Staff can be a second set of eyes, watch your drink while you're in the restroom to ensure nothing goes into it except what was mixed behind the bar, and arrange for transportation or an escort by staff should things go sideways. You can also ask them to make all your drinks nonalcoholic after that first round to avoid any awkward discussions about drinking. And you want to know what I think this staff insider tip is? It's special operations at its finest: clandestine, simple, and effective.

Be armed. No kidding. C'mon, you've read Tool 1, you should be anyway. That Mace or tactical pen is at the ready for when you decide to leave early because he or she is radiating "stalker." Where this can be most critical is when it's time to walk out from your date or go in separate directions. Put your hand in your pocket, purse, backpack, Indiana Jones satchel, whatever, but have your hand on your self-defense tool. Pulling it out and palming it is better still. Do this until you know you're in a safe place or have reached a safe distance. If they've walked you to your car or metro stop (never your home because... you know why) you're ready in the event they attempt a forced entry, even if they seem great.

Dial in your Intuition. Think about it before you go on your date. Review and reinforce the things you know about your Intuition insofar as what you know works best for you. Then be sure to listen to your inner voice while listening to their captivating story about how they raise prizewinning zucchini. This is especially important if you're not enjoying yourself or picking up any signal you don't like. If she or he is radiating "stalker," that's your signal. Watch for body language from Rule 2. Also, if they're not interested in you or what you have to say, it could be they're just self-centered egoists but it could also be a sign that they don't see you as a human and therefore possibly are assessing you as prey. An easy reveal is the asymmetrical contemptuous smirk.

When in doubt or bored, bail. When you know it's not going to work or you aren't interested, take that cue and your leave. You don't owe the other person anything. It's a common social obligation not to let other people down. It's also difficult to tell someone you're not interested or don't think you're a good match. But it's better to make a definite statement about how you feel than to mislead someone through politeness. Don't be afraid to say, "You're great but I just don't think we have enough in common. I'm going to go now." Or, "I'm not the person you're looking for. Thanks for a great _____ [whatever]. I've enjoyed meeting you and take care." No need to say you're sorry ever. There's nothing to be sorry for. Just tell them it's not right for you. That's a socially acceptable and polite way to extricate yourself. If you sense tension or suspect you might get a Joe Keesling response as you disentangle yourself, it's important to be prepared for that adverse reaction in advance. If it comes, be direct and terminate it on the spot succinctly and without engaging them further. A simple "I'm leaving" as you stand works. And after you've left, your SA radar should be on high alert until you're safely home.

TOOL SIX

TRAVEL PLANNING

Nairobi, Kenya

IN 2012, CIA CASE OFFICER VICTORIA WAS TASKED WITH COMBATING Xarakada Mujaahidiinta Alshabaab, a Somali terrorist organization better known by its Anglicized name al-Shabaab. Literally translated, the group's name means "movement of striving youth," an almost Orwellian title for an organization that has repeatedly spilled violence and religious vitriol across its shared border with Kenya and other neighboring countries. Though she was based in the US, Victoria was working a Kenyan source connected to the group whom she needed to meet in person, which meant traveling to Kenya's capital, Nairobi. Al-Shabaab was highly active in Kenya at the time, planning attacks in response to a Kenyan-led operation in Somalia earlier in the year.

Because she was working undercover at the time, much of Victoria's planning took place in her home in the US. She would be visiting Kenya ostensibly as a female tourist traveling alone. She'd learned to cover her military background and the subtleties that transmitted by reverting to her origins. "Anyone who thought I might have been prior military, I'd just tell them, 'Of course I'm aggressive and talk fast with my hands, I'm a New Yorker. It's in the water; it's in the bagels.'"

And though she'd be traveling alone to Kenya, in actuality all of her advance planning was done for two. Victoria, it turns out, was pregnant with her first child. Five months pregnant. "So, in addition to the usual concerns of traveling as a lone female and undercover, I was concerned for my baby and avoiding things like malaria and hepatitis, parasites in the water and foodborne diseases in addition to rampant street crime and al-Shabaab."

Because she lived under what's referred to as "commercial cover," Victoria lived like a civilian and no one knew she was a CIA case officer except her husband, himself a contract CIA employee, and coworkers with the need to know. "My parents never knew about my career until after I left the agency. No one in my family had ever even held a gun." Because of that she was basically self-reliant in making safe travel plans, just like you.

Says Victoria, "The tools you need to safely plan don't require access to CIA files. Really, the best place to start is online. But you need to get below the surface (Wikipedia), find blogs, learn what people are saying about your destination." And that's precisely what she did, beginning with Travelocity, the travel website. The wider your search and the deeper you dig, the greater your information and the better your plan will be for getting around safely. "People want to tell their stories, and if they have a bad time they'll let you know." From them you can glean where and when places are safe and when they're not. Because she had to conduct day-long SDRs and also find meeting locations that would not draw attention to herself or risk her (and her baby's) safety in addition to ensuring she didn't compromise her source, the search became highly detailed. You, dear reader, do not have those problems.

Once in Kenya, she moved from the internet to the human network. And because she was undercover as a tourist, she'd be visiting tourist destinations. "You feel obligated, of course, to get the best bang for the taxpayer's buck . . ." She'd repeat her search for locations and routes but in addition used the knowledge base of the locals. Concierges, cabdrivers, restaurant employees, or groups of other tourists (as a lone female she would never approach men, whether in groups or as individuals) are great sources. From a preplanning standpoint, that is to say before you depart the safety of your home, hotel, or car, a particularly good question to ask is, "Are there any places I shouldn't go?" a very different proposition than "Where should I go?"

Before leaving her hotel, Victoria would outline her plan each day, sometimes even days in advance, and incorporate all the knowledge she gleaned online and from locals, and the accumulated knowledge of her time in-country. For several weeks she navigated through Nairobi's less glamorous neighborhoods in addition to her (slightly) higher-profile tourist stops at better-known shopping centers and attractions. At the end of her trip she returned, mission accomplished and safe. Her son was born four months later.

Three weeks after Victoria left Nairobi, four al-Shabaab terrorists seized the sprawling Westgate shopping center, a popular spot with tourists and locals alike, holding it captive while simultaneously executing hostages. Two hundred victims, seventy-one of them fatalities, were left in the aftermath of the day-long siege. Had Victoria been there during that time it's doubtful she would have crossed paths with the perpetrators—she avoided Westgate precisely because she was undercover and it was an extremely high-profile location.

PREPLANNING

Victoria's Kenyan deployment provides textbook examples of what to do, from hotel selection to tourist activities. However, preplans needn't be mapped out like a clandestine CIA deployment to an African country subject to terrorist attacks. Rather, preplanning should be a habit you develop. When making reservations for your next vacation, don't stop with airfare and hotel selection, spend time and use the resources and checklists contained in the appendices.

The single greatest benefit to preplanning is your ability to do it from the comfort of home. Or in your hotel before going out for the day or on to another destination. In doing so, you can consider things you might not think of once you're out and about. Knowing such things as the location of the closest hospital or available urgent care makes a difference. Where are the local police and what's their number? Where's the closest US consulate?

If you travel to Paris, Mexico City, or Hanoi with little forethought, you shouldn't be surprised if you inadvertently find yourself in a bad situation wondering, "What do we do now?" Advance planning for contingencies is never a wasted effort. Knowledge is power and, more specifically in this context, safety.

DESTINATION ASSESSMENT

The first step in travel planning is to understand the situation at your destination. Use government websites to determine threats and plan for emergencies. Australia's Smartraveller site is my favorite because it's the easiest to navigate and their layout is super intuitive. You needn't be an Aussie to use it. Regardless, visit your country's official site so you can obtain phone numbers and locations for emergency government assistance.

I also suggest digging deeper than foreign office or State Department pages. As Victoria suggests, search out blogs, online magazine articles, and travel-specific sites for the type of activities you're interested in (such as shopping, adventure travel, or ecotourism) and see what they offer.

Use your research to separate reality from the hype. Here's an example: Violence in Mexico. Despite its bad rap, Mexico has roughly 15 firearm homicides per 100,000 people vs. 120 per 100,000 in the US. However, vehicle and belongings thefts are relatively frequent in Mexico compared to the States—as I so painfully and embarrassingly learned. Express kidnapping (holding you until you ransom yourself by withdrawing cash from an ATM, for instance) and robbery are also a common type of crime, though more so in urban centers than at resorts. By knowing these details rather than listening to propaganda or rumor, you can understand the real risks involved in your trip. This isn't paranoia—merely prudence. Only then can you grasp the personal risk vs. reward. In the end, you're still responsible for your own choices, so not short-changing your ability to get the most complete picture is a wise proposition.

Tourist Destinations

Just as Victoria did, use your internet savvy to identify hot spots and common destinations. Some major locations, such as the Colosseum in Rome, or popular parts of certain cities such as Soho in London or Times Square in New York City, collect criminals of various varieties and at different times of year and even times of day or evening. What you need to know beforehand is that you should be on heightened alert. Refer back to your SA, and in any place that attracts tourists, whether crowded during popular times or deserted in poor weather or late at night, you should be Attentively Aware at all times. It's not paranoia to elevate your attention in environments where you're more likely to be targeted.

A few words on the subjects of immobilization and kidnapping, two topics that repeatedly came to my attention in the course of interviews and feedback while writing this book. There is not some magic bullet or special set of considerations that prevent restraint or kidnapping. That's because defending against them is not separate or uniquely different from other types of crimes in preventing the act before it happens. Kidnappings occur in the same places as other crimes. It's merely a crime categorization and from a defense standpoint no different than robbery or sexual assault. Prevention starts with your Situational Awareness and Intuition and finishes with preventative action and regrouping.

EMERGENCIES

Know how and when to contact authorities before you depart for your trip, not after you arrive at your destination—the latter is tantamount to planning contingencies *after* you've launched a combat mission into enemy territory. You need not be a veteran to understand that's a bad idea. Planning for your personal safety is a habit and, in worst-case scenarios where you need the authorities or medical facilities, can save a life when seconds count. At a minimum, know where hospitals or medical care facilities are located in relation to your hotel and also how to immediately dial the police.

If everything goes haywire while you're in a foreign country, such as 2020's COVID-19 outbreak, for instance, or there's a severe earthquake or even a national crisis (most people don't know that Thailand has experienced multiple military coups—I witnessed the violence firsthand when red shirts vs. yellow shirts was raging in Bangkok in 2008), you need to know where to go if suddenly the internet or phone service drop. Your embassy, whatever your country of citizenship, is the surest source of information and security when all else fails.

HOTELS

First, never use a hotel's or resort's website to determine its safety. On their site everything is always great. That's marketing. It's fine for assessing amenities but pointless as far as safety. A Google search using their property's name, address, or neighborhood can reveal incidents or trends the hotel would rather you not know about. You can then use that to make a better assessment of your safety or in deciding whether to choose that location. In Jamaica there was a long string of sexual assaults at a number of up-scale resort properties, sometimes committed by employees, that went unreported until enough numbers surfaced to raise public awareness. I'm not suggesting you avoid that particular Caribbean destination; however, over a two-year period it became obvious hotels were suppressing the frequency and severity of assaults on their properties in an attempt to protect business. Google Jamaica/resort/sexual assault and you'll get a string of articles from those years. Wouldn't you like to know about that before you go there?

It's common practice in the special operations and clandestine communities to pick a certain type of room. Don't get one that has access to the outside or ground floor. The second through sixth floors are optimal (ground floors are too easily penetrated and above the sixth is harder to evacuate in the event of fire or terrorist attack). Use the hotel checklists in Appendix B when you make your reservation. If you're reserving online, it's harder to determine certain things such as types of locks and hours of restricted entry. I suggest dialing the hotel directly to ensure they've got what you need. You can always get off the phone and make your reservation through your favorite site afterward to accumulate or redeem those all-important "points."

CONCLUSION

Travel planning for safety is primarily about thinking in advance, not in reaction to the environment or culture you're in. It needn't be complex or something you must be well versed in by memory. There are many resources available to you for free, from government websites to travel agencies and specialized destination or travel websites as well as the appendices in this book. Regardless of where you get your information, the more you dig into your intended location, its potential for crime or other threats (such as health or climatic), cultural peculiarities, and your planned activities, the less likely you are to be surprised by something unpleasant. And isn't the freedom to explore without worry what travel is all about?

AFTERWORD

This book is by no means a comprehensive solution to every threat or a one-size-fits-all answer for safety considerations. However, my hope is that these pages provide a new perspective and instill greater faith in your own awareness and innate abilities to prevent problems before they start or effectively avoid them when you're confronted by threatening individuals or dangerous situations.

Use each rule as it's meant to be used, starting with the dual foundation of Situational Awareness and Intuition. Let those shape your understanding of whatever environment you find yourself in. Using both is the means by which you'll "Know." Knowing in turn will allow you to determine if you have a problem. And if so, that is your catalyst for making a deliberate or hasty plan. Problem determination and crisis planning is how you'll be "Prepared." So that, should the time come, you can "Act," decisively and appropriately, both in the crisis and its aftermath. Your final step, in the event of an incident, is to "Recover." Draw on those you trust and love, or consult experts so that you can move on along the path of your life. Know, Prepare, Act. Those are the three pillars and, as you now understand, are easily remembered when you think of them as sequential.

While this book is based on extensive experience and expertise, don't rely on experts for all your advice. Think for yourself. Apply what you've learned here and then modify it, shape it to fit your own particular circumstances and needs. Find other sources of information and spend time thinking about how to apply them to your personal safety. I've included resources in the appendices expressly for that reason. But even those are just that: resources. They are merely starting or reference points for mapping your own path. And remember, all the exercises in the book are also available for free on my website under the Power of Awareness section to either print or view on your phone, just not while you're walking...

In my own life I've learned a great deal about personal responsibility by immersing myself in Buddhism during the few years that I had the good fortune to work and travel in Thailand and Southeast Asia. The one thing I've taken away that was central to Siddhartha Gautama's (the man who came to be known as the Buddha) teachings was, "Don't take anyone's word for it. You have to figure life out for yourself." He was a wise man. And in the end, the rules and tools I created and put in this book are simply here to help you figure things out for yourself.

In life, crises come and go. Our lives move on, and over time events recede into our past. Traumatic events never truly disappear but they do dim. The edges surrounding them soften and become less sharp. That's certainly my personal experience with trauma and violence. One of the stories I encountered through my research for this book, and that continues to inspire me, is the case of Carol DaRonch, the "girl who got away." Even though Ted Bundy periodically occupied her life for fifteen years through the trials and the course of his convictions and eventual execution, when it was over, she moved on. She came to understand that he was no longer a part of her reality in going forward. Happiness isn't the best revenge in my opinion. It's better than revenge because it needn't be expressed in terms of opposition to something else. It's merely happiness. And everyone deserves that.

Sometimes, if we do things correctly and are lucky, situations we think might turn out violently or simply differently than we'd like can resolve themselves. One such case from my own history is that of the near bar fight between my buddies in the Alan Parsons Project band and Bruce Lee Junior and his sidekick Sleeve Tattoo. So, what happened in the event? Nothing, as it turned out. By de-escalating the problem and not feeding into Bruce's desire for a fistfight, we gave his drug-addled attention time to turn elsewhere, as I knew it would. In fact, in the course of the third quarter of the Super Bowl he developed an ersatz fraternal bond with guitarist Dan Tracey, who had begun dispensing parenting advice (Bruce was a dad), so much so that when Sleeve Tattoo got out of line (no doubt thanks to a second gram of coke) during the fourth quarter, it was Bruce who put his own companion in his place. But the lesson here isn't that the situation resolved itself through patience, it's that I recognized the potential greater threat for what it was and was prepared with a plan and appropriate actions if it didn't. Fortunately, it never came to that.

Regarding my mistake in Mexico: Our chase truck, race car, and belongings disappeared. However, within forty-eight hours of the theft, the thieves who'd stolen our possessions did the natural thing and turned on all the electronics. We had an embedded GPS tracking device in one (some special operations habits die hard), so when they turned it on, we were able to pin their coordinates to within a single block in the urban sprawl of Tijuana by correlating them with overhead satellite imagery. Leveraging a Navy SEAL contact who had links to the Mexican military, we pre-staged forces for a potential raid. It was an impressive feat of coordination in a country that took an hour for the police to even respond to our theft. The Mexican authorities managed to send us a photo of the front of a red Ford pickup similar to ours backed under an awning and stuffed behind some other cars in one compound. It was a promising sign.

The Mexican Army swooped into the neighborhood in a predawn raid. When they did, the GPS signal went dark, indicating the thieves were savvier than it might have seemed at first. Soldiers raided a few compounds they deemed likely, but with no signal it was impossible to find the device without an exhaustive door-to-door search, something the Mexicans weren't willing to do. A reasonable conclusion on their part. The signal never reappeared, nothing was ever heard of our possessions again, and $100,000 in specialized vehicles vanished into the Mexican underworld. It was a costly and bitter lesson for a special operations expert with a three-decade track record of no losses. Proving yet again that no one is immune.

As for Billy, my former operator who was so fortunate to survive the assassin that started this book? I'm happy to report he made it safely to retirement and now lives with his family in the Midwest, a most stalwart believer in listening to one's Intuition.

There are both lesser and greater evils lurking around us and you needn't be a CIA spy, police detective, or SOF operator to know that Ted Bundy is not the only asshole wandering the planet. We can't rid the world of all of them, but by using the skills you've learned you can avoid encounters and confrontations altogether. And also remember that crises are not about playing fair. To paraphrase the late great W. C. Fields, never give an asshole an even break.

Know that the absence of confrontation and crises means you're doing things correctly because nothing has happened. There are times in my own life, walking the evening streets of a city or operating in third-world hot spots, when I know I've narrowly avoided bad situations and others when I'm sure I've no idea how close I even came. You'll never know what you narrowly avoided for the same reason that you can't prove a negative, but that doesn't mean you haven't accomplished your goal of moving about the world safely, just the opposite in fact. And in that respect, there is no difference between those of us who are experts and everyone else. We're all the same.

With the information you've learned you're now armed to go about your typical day at home and forward in the world a more confident and prepared person. You now know the most powerful tool is your Power of Awareness. Power of Awareness equals safety and security, which in turn equals confidence. That well-placed confidence equals personal power, pure and simple.

Know that you're no longer the inviting target bad guys are looking for, but one of the few who travel with your eyes open and your mind ready for whatever you may encounter. My sincere hope is that this book saves a life. It is the reason I wrote it.

The world is a fascinating and wondrous place. Meant to be explored and experienced with those you love and cherish, from your front door to the far side of the planet. May you enjoy your home and travels with confidence.

ACKNOWLEDGMENTS

The genesis for these words was my agent Larry Weissman, who'd hounded me to write them for several years because he thought it was a necessary book. I repeatedly refused because I was interested in other subjects, until one fateful day while standing atop a Mexican mountain... To both my literary agents, Larry and his wife, Sascha Alper, thank you for your encouragement, superior representation, and dear friendship. Thanks also to my super Hollywood agent, Josie Freedman.

At Grand Central: My editor Maddie Caldwell, thanks for your shared vision and belief in the power of awareness to change lives and keep people safe and your tireless efforts to improve my voice and bring the perspective of the audience I hoped most to reach. My good friend and production editor Mari Okuda, who goes above the call patiently remedying my dangling participles, omissions, and inconsistencies, and also knows the best places to eat in Manhattan. Thanks also to Jacqui Young for her coordination and to Rick Ball for an exceptional copyedit. To the entire Grand Central team that shape, promote, sell, and support my continued dream as a full-time writer, a heartfelt thank-you.

The following were early readers and offered many suggestions: Casey Baker, Dave Bock, Rika N. Jain, Grace and Glen Kwon, John Nightingale, Dave Richards, Natalie St. Denis, John Schilling. For mountain seclusion, thanks to Amy and Bo Huggins.

ACKNOWLEDGMENTS

At CIA, thanks to Victoria and Frank for sharing stories and expertise. From the SOF community, thanks to Billy and Dutch for sharing war stories and for our years of service together and Calvin Longton for martial expertise (www.precisionmartialarts.com—in Navarre, FL, stop by, tell him Dano sent you). From LAPD, thank you to the husband-and-wife team of Detectives Starsky and Hutch, who exemplify commitment to helping people recover from the tragedy of crime, and also for hosting me during my research. Thanks to FBI agents Grant Mendenhall and Tim Swanson for connections far and wide. A. J. DeAndrea was essential in making sense of the travesty that is active shooters. To Ogden PD Chief Randy Watt, who connected me to Amber Stell and to Amber for insights into victim recovery. Thank you especially to the anonymous survivors and other sources who remain unnamed. Much appreciation to my talented stepson Zach Spilinek for my website.

Finally, my wife, Julie, whose intelligence career at NSA was something to behold (for those of us with access) and to whom this book is dedicated, for the safety she and the rest of that agency have thanklessly provided for all Americans. Thank you for being my idea co-conspirator, first and last editor, globetrotting partner, and allowing me to pursue my dream of being a writer. As always, words cannot express my love and admiration.

Appendix A

RESOURCES

ACTIVE SHOOTER AND MASS ATTACKS IN CROWDED AND PUBLIC SPACES:

Department of Homeland Security resources:

https://www.dhs.gov/cisa/active-shooter-preparedness

- Provides information on how to prepare for an active shooter and what to do if you find yourself in an active shooting event.

https://www.dhs.gov/xlibrary/assets/active_shooter_booklet.pdf

- Key information for how to respond in an active shooter event, including emergency numbers beyond 9-1-1 (e.g., FBI Field Office, facility security, local hospitals), what to tell 9-1-1 dispatchers, practices for coping with an active shooter situation, and immediate steps to take.

https://www.ready.gov/active-shooter

- Provides information and descriptions of what to do if you find yourself in an active shooting event.

https://www.ready.gov/public-spaces

- Understanding mass attacks, recognizing the warning signs, and steps to take if you find yourself in a mass-attack event.

I Love U Guys Foundation:

http://iloveyouguys.org/index.html#home

- Founded in the wake of the 2006 Platte Canyon High School shooting, I Love U Guys provides schools and businesses with planning materials and can also deliver training.

ASSAULTS

Domestic Violence

For resources by state, visit the US Department of Health & Human Services' Office on Women's Health, https://www.womenshealth.gov/relationships-and-safety/get -help/state-resources.

National Center on Domestic Violence, Trauma & Mental Health, http://www.nationalcenterdvtraumamh.org/resources /national-domestic-violence-organizations.

National Coalition Against Domestic Violence, https://ncadv.org.

National Domestic Violence Hotline, https://www.thehotline.org, 1-800-799-7233.

Protection Order information can be found at https://www.womenslaw.org.

Sexual Assault

International Rape Crisis Hotlines can be found at http://www.ibiblio.org/rcip/internl.html.

National Sexual Assault Telephone Hotline, 800-656-HOPE (4673), https://www.rainn.org/ (contains national and inter-national resources).

National Sexual Violence Resource Center,
https://www.nsvrc.org.

Victims of sexual assault while abroad can call the US Department of State, Office of Overseas Citizens Services at +1-202-501-4444 (from overseas) or 1-888-407-4747 (in the US).

Victims can also contact their local embassy or consulate to navigate local laws and find resources,
https://www.usembassy.gov.

Teen Dating Violence/Healthy Relationships for Teens

National Teen Dating Abuse Helpline, 1-866-331-9474 or 1-866-331-8453 (TTY), https://www.loveisrespect.org.

Trauma and Children

Childhelp National Child Abuse Hotline, 1-800-422-4453,
https://www.childhelp.org/hotline.

National Child Traumatic Stress Network,
https://www.nctsn.org.

IDENTITY THEFT

Federal government identity-theft resources:

https://www.identitytheft.gov

https://identitytheft.gov/Top-Company-Contacts

- What to do if your personal information is stolen (e.g., wallet, purse, or electronic device containing Personally Identifiable Information [PII]).

- The Federal Trade Commission (FTC), the nation's consumer protection agency, provides centralized information to report and help resolve financial issues and other problems that can result from identity theft. You'll find helpful links to the Social Security Administration, Internal Revenue Service (IRS), Department of Justice, Department of State, and many more.

- Two key forms to fill out and submit:

  - https://www.irs.gov/pub/irs-pdf/f14039.pdf, an Identity Theft Affidavit form, will alert the IRS to the identity theft and they will mark your tax account with an identity-theft indicator. This will help stop thieves from using your information to file a fraudulent return. Use this form if your Social Security number was stolen along with other identifying information needed to file a tax return, such as your full name and address.

- ° https://eforms.state.gov/Forms/ds64.pdf, a Statement Regarding a Lost or Stolen US Passport Book and/or Card, which is required before obtaining a replacement passport, even if working overseas with a US consular office.

TRAVEL RESOURCES, SAFETY, AND OTHER CONSIDERATIONS

If you are a victim of a crime overseas:

https://travel.state.gov/content/travel/en/international-travel /emergencies/crime.html

- Provides specific information for those who are victims of a crime overseas, such as what the State Department can and cannot do and how they can help, with resources and contacts by country, including embassy and consulates, replacement of stolen passports, addressing emergency needs that arise as a result of the crime, and so forth.

Know the location of the nearest US Embassy and Consulate:

https://www.usembassy.gov

- Central resource for websites of US Embassies, Consulates, and Diplomatic Missions around the world.

Additional safety tips to keep you safe while traveling abroad:

Australian Smartraveller

https://www.smartraveller.gov.au

British Foreign Office travel advice

https://www.gov.uk/foreign-travel-advice

https://www.usa.gov/americans-abroad#item-36137

- Helpful resources for Americans planning travel outside the US, including Trusted Traveler Programs, emergency assistance abroad, and driving outside the US.

Emergencies While Abroad

**https://travel.state.gov/content/travel/en/international-travel
/emergencies.html**

- Specific information for what to do if you are overseas and in
need of emergency assistance.

*State Department country-specific safety and security (travel
alerts):*

https://travel.state.gov/destination

- Provides country-specific details that can affect travel such as
entry/exit requirements, local laws and customs, health conditions, transportation, and other relevant information.

State Department international travel resources:

**https://travel.state.gov/content/travel/en/international-travel
/before-you-go/helpfultravelresources.html**

- "Know Before You Go"—Provides several helpful travel resources,
including safety messaging, the free Smart Traveler Enrollment
Program (STEP), checklists, and information on driving and road
safety abroad.

RESOURCES

Traveler-specific information:

https://travel.state.gov/content/travel/en/international-travel /before-you-go/travelers-with-special-considerations.html

- Considerations and travel resources for various types of travelers such as faith-based, women, pilgrimage (e.g., Hajj), travelers with disabilities, LGBTQ, cruise ships, high-risk areas, older travelers, US volunteers abroad, travelers with pets, and travelers with firearms.

Appendix B

CHECKLISTS

PRE-TRAVEL CHECKLIST

☐ <u>Know before you go</u>—This cannot be emphasized enough. Research your destination before you arrive. At a minimum, check the US State Department's website to be aware of any potential security issues. Another official site I recommend is Australia's Smartraveller website.

☐ Enroll in the State Department's Smart Traveler Enrollment Program to receive security and emergency alerts about your destination. Look up the addresses and phone numbers of the local US Embassy or Consulate and keep them with you at all times.

☐ Scan and save an electronic copy of important documents, including passports, medical insurance cards, itineraries, travel insurance, and visas before you depart. Email the file to yourself so you have it available if your information is lost or stolen.

☐ Obtain travel insurance. In the event of theft or robbery, your stolen valuables often are covered and can be replaced. If you are injured or attacked, your medical bills will be covered.

☐ Ensure you have a cell phone and plan that work in your destination country. Make sure you have the proper chargers/adapters and keep your phone at full battery. Bring a portable battery charger so you have power for phones on the go.

☐ Download maps onto tablets and phones so you can view them offline.

☐ Keep family and friends updated. Ensure they have a copy of your itinerary and you establish a check-in schedule so they can keep tabs on your whereabouts for your safety.

☐ Don't bring unnecessary items—credit cards that you won't use, identification you don't need—or risky items (such as keys you regularly carry in a purse). Only bring documents, identification, cards, etc., that you absolutely must have.

☐ Diversify your finances. Don't rely exclusively on digital currency. Traveler's checks are out of fashion but can be replaced if stolen. Round them out with some cash for "sketchy" vendors or bargaining on the street. Do not use credit cards if your Intuition is going off.

☐ Book hotel rooms online. It'll save time when you arrive, and you have to give less information over the counter when checking in.

☐ Don't carry everything together. Separate monetary and identifying items you must carry on you, and carry them in different places on your person. This will prevent you from losing everything if your wallet or purse gets stolen. Don't ever carry anything in your back pockets, including hotel room keys.

HOTEL CHECKLISTS

Hotel selection checklist:

☐ Is the area crime free or acceptable?

☐ Are emergency exits and doors locked during the hours the hotel says they are?

☐ Do you need a key to open them?

☐ Are exits well lit?

☐ Do alternate and emergency exits have enough open space that you can't get ambushed using them after hours?

☐ Are parking areas secure or at least well lit?

☐ Ensure parking garage elevators do not access room floors directly.

☐ Ensure room phones can dial outside numbers directly (such as for police).

Checking-in checklist:

☐ Do not allow your luggage to be separated from you until you've registered or it's signed for by a bellhop or the front counter.

☐ Don't leave credit cards or wallets on the counter while checking in. Hand over any identification and wait for the employee to take it from you. When they hand it back, put it away, *then* complete any registration. It's easy to leave a card or wallet behind, especially if you've been traveling.

☐ Ask for two hotel business cards. Keep them on you to use with taxis or in the event of an emergency while away from your room. This saves you from trying to remember information while under duress or while hailing a taxi in a foreign language or unfamiliar city.

☐ If you're a woman traveling alone, check in as Mr. and Mrs. so people get the idea that you're not alone. Get two room keys.

☐ Confirm that the hotel should not forward calls to your room. Instead, ask them to ring you from the front desk with any inquiries.

☐ If you're a woman traveling alone, feel free to ask someone at the front desk or a bellhop to accompany you in the elevator, especially in large hotels.

☐ Always enter an elevator last so you can observe everyone else. This also allows you to select your floor last and to see if someone decides to "conveniently" follow you on your floor. If they do, pretend you left something downstairs and get back in the elevator.

☐ If you feel you're being followed/stalked, go to the floor above your room. That way the stalker will think you're staying on that floor.

☐ Write down your name and phone number and hand them over with a printout of your reservation, a copy of your passport, and whatever you're using to pay for the room (e.g., a credit card). This helps prevent eavesdroppers from collecting personal information.

Hotel room selection checklist:

☐ Select a room between the second and sixth floors if possible. If not, go higher, never ground floor.

☐ Does the entry door have at least two physical locks (in addition to needing a key)?

☐ Is the door solid?

☐ Does any adjoining room have at least one physical lock?

☐ Does your balcony have at least two physical locks?

☐ Does the balcony prevent someone from climbing onto yours from an adjacent room or different floor? Can they reach your balcony from the ground by climbing up?

☐ Do any windows prevent someone from climbing through them?

☐ Do the windows lock securely?

☐ Sleep with the windows and balcony door closed unless you're 100 percent confident they cannot be used for entry.

☐ "Do not disturb" should always be on display. Contact the front desk or housekeeping directly and let them know when you'll be wanting service/cleaning.

In the Room

☐ The dead bolt and the latch bolt should be engaged as soon as you enter.

☐ Purchase a safety doorstop you can place against the door, and use it whenever you're inside. A common tactic is for thieves to break in when they hear the shower.

☐ Turn on the television at low volume but loud enough to hear at the door if someone's listening, when you leave the room.

☐ When someone comes to the door, never open it to ascertain who it is. If you ordered room service, be sure to ask who the order is for before opening.

HOME SECURITY ASSESSMENT

Home security checklist:

Walk around your home from the outside. If you wanted to break in, how would you do it? If you'd watched your home/apartment/condo for a few weeks, when would you do it? Think about this from the standpoint of someone who wants your stuff and therefore has no desire to confront you. Then consider it from the standpoint of Ted Bundy, American asshole. Make some notes and think about them, then use this checklist to assess weak points and address them.

Doors

Doors are the first entry point into your home for intruders. If you don't have solid doors, invest in dead bolts that extend into the frame (most residential dead bolts anchor only to the strike plate and can be kicked in by a fairly determined preteen). Be aware that most common locks installed in homes are easily picked. Consider brands that emphasize their security over convenience. If your doors are not solid, consider having a floor-mounted security doorstop installed.

☐ Are exterior doors solid wood or reinforced metal so they can withstand battering?

☐ Does your front door have a dead bolt separate from the key lock?

☐ Does the front door dead bolt extend three inches (eight centimeters) into the frame of the structure?

☐ Check other exterior doors for the same.

☐ If you have a garage, is the door leading inside solid and does it have a dead bolt?

☐ If there are windows within forty inches (100 cm) of your front door, you need to consult a locksmith about installing double-cylinder-style dead bolts to prevent reach-arounds.

☐ If you have sliding glass doors to a patio, are they double-locked?

☐ Are doorways well lit so intruders are exposed if they're attempting to gain entry?

☐ Do you have peepholes or windows that allow you to see who's at the front door?

☐ If you have a garage door, can it be forced open, either by overcoming the opener motor or because you don't have one?

☐ Does your garage door with opener have a lock that overrides the openers? (Most openers now have rolling codes, but if yours doesn't, you need to know the code can be captured.)

Windows

Every window should be considered as a vulnerability, sometimes from as unexpected a source as the neighboring apartment. If windows are reachable from the ground, the roof, a ladder, or even a tree, that must be addressed. Most residential window locks are not heavy duty and can be jimmied or overcome.

☐ Do entry-vulnerable windows have solid locks? Or can you overcome/defeat them by pushing with determination? (Don't break your window locks, but when you do this test, ask yourself, *could* you do it?)

☐ Do you have window air conditioners that could be removed and then the opening climbed through or the window opened by reaching around?

☐ Is your original Van Gogh or priceless unicorn figurine collection visible from the outside? If so, consider how to mask or place them so they don't serve as enticements.

Other exterior considerations:

☐ Do you have motion sensor lights?

☐ Are there timed lights that illuminate areas of vulnerability?

☐ Do you have a spare key hidden someplace stupid? (Sorry, but if you have it under the mat, above the jamb, or in that lone obviously fake rock, you're asking for your unicorn figurines to be lifted.)

☐ Do you have a security system? Is it truly monitored? If so, have you tested it? Do they respond or do the cops show up? (You can always claim ignorance, but the peace of mind is worth the false alarm. Just don't tell them I said so.)

☐ Is there a crawl space or floor-level gap or even a basement entry area that makes your home vulnerable?

Door, window, and exterior notes:

Sliding and standard windows can be easily and cheaply reinforced using ¾" or 1" wooden dowels obtained from any home supply store and laying them in the track. If you measure them, they'll often cut them to length for free. A trick I like to use if you need that window or sliding door to be open a few inches or centimeters for ventilation is to have them cut that much off the total length. When you want the door or window open, simply remove the short piece and voilà! You're ventilated and secure. Simply replace the short piece when you want to close and lock up.

Sliding doors can also be secured in the ventilation open position with pins that are drilled through the frame and slide. However, if you have this done, it needs to be at the far end of the door away from the opening to prevent reach-arounds.

Do you have a trusted neighbor for a spare key? If not, you need to spend some time on a quality place to hide one. One of my favorites was a false pop-up sprinkler that you placed in the ground.

For viewing your front and back entries, consider Ring or another company that provides the ability to observe who's around or has been there, while you're at home or remotely. Do not scrimp with this and remember, they too can be hacked.

If you don't have a security system (or don't live in a doorman-manned apartment in Manhattan), get one. If you can't afford one, get a sign. You're not here to play fair.

It should go without saying but . . . do you lock doors and windows and other vulnerable entry points every time you leave or go to bed? If not, hello Ted . . .

SELECTED BIBLIOGRAPHY

BOOKS

De Becker, G. (1998). *The gift of fear: And other survival signals that protect us from violence*. Dell.

Duke, A. (2018). *Thinking in bets: Making smarter decisions when you don't have all the facts*. Portfolio/Penguin.

Gladwell, M. (2005). *Blink: The power of thinking without thinking*. Little, Brown.

Turner, K. A. (2015). *Radical remission: Surviving cancer against all odds*. HarperOne.

Wrangham, R. W., and Peterson, D. (1996). *Demonic males: Apes and the origins of human violence*. Houghton Mifflin Harcourt.

ARTICLES AND DOCUMENTS

America grapples with a lethal mix of terrorism and lax gun laws. (2019, August 8). *The Economist*. https://www.economist.com/united-states/2019/08/08/america-grapples-with-a-lethal-mix-of-terrorism-and-lax-gun-laws

Book, A., Costello, K., and Camilleri, J. A. (2013). Psychopathy and victim selection: The use of gait as a cue to vulnerability. *Journal of Interpersonal Violence*, *28*(11), 2368–2383. https://doi.org/10.1177/0886260512475315

Carlson, A. (2019, February 6). The true story of Ted Bundy's "girl who got away": Teen put him behind bars—and her life now. *People*. https://people.com/crime/true-story-carol-daronch-now-ted-bundy-movie/

Denardo Roney, J. L., and Falkenbach, D. M. (2018, January 18). Psychopathy and victim selection: Does nonverbal decoding or empathy impact vulnerability ratings? *Journal of Interpersonal Violence*. https://journals.sagepub.com/doi/10.1177/0886260517742914

Gunns, R. E., Johnston, L., and Hudson, S. M. (2002). Victim selection and kinematics: A point-light investigation of vulnerability to attack. *Journal of Nonverbal Behavior*, *26*, 129–158. https://link.springer.com/article/10.1023/A:1020744915533

Parks, Bernard C. (1998, June 12). Report on North Hollywood bank robbery to

Honorable Board of Police Commissioners. Intradepartmental Correspondence OIS #18-97

Silverstein, J. (2019, July 31). Mass shootings in U.S. 2019: There were more mass shootings than days in 2019. CBSNews.com. https://www.cbsnews.com/news /mass-shootings-2019-more-than-days-365/

Turner, K. (2014, May 20). The science behind intuition: Why you should trust your gut. *Psychology Today*. https://www.psychologytoday.com/us/blog/radical -remission/201405/the-science-behind-intuition

WEBSITES

Graduate Institute of International and Development Studies, Geneva, Switzerland. (2019). *Small Arms Survey*. http://www.smallarmssurvey.org

Gun Violence Archive. (2020). https://www.gunviolencearchive.org

Mass Shooting Tracker. (2020). https://www.massshootingtracker.site/about/

National Weather Service. (2020). How dangerous is lightning? https://www.weather .gov/safety/lightning-odds

Stanford University Libraries. (2020). Mass shootings in America. https://library .stanford.edu/projects/mass-shootings-america

World Population Review. (2020). Mass shootings by country 2020. https://world populationreview.com/country-rankings/mass-shootings-by-country/

INDEX

INDEX

INDEX

INDEX